RUUD GULLIT
My Autobiography

RUUD GULLIT
My Autobiography

Ruud Gullit

Published by Century in 1998

3 5 7 9 10 8 6 4 2

Copyright © Ruud Gullit 1998

Ruud Gullit has asserted his right under the Copyright, Designs
and Patents Act, 1988, to be identified as the author of this work

First published in the United Kingdom in 1998 by Century
Random House UK Limited
20 Vauxhall Bridge Road, London SW1V 2SA

Random House Australia (Pty) Limited
20 Alfred Street, Milsons Point, Sydney,
New South Wales 2061, Australia

Random House New Zealand Limited
18 Poland Road, Glenfield,
Auckland 10, New Zealand

Random House South Africa (Pty) Limited
Endulini, 5a Jubilee Road, Parktown 2193, South Africa

Random House UK Limited Reg. No. 954009

A CIP catalogue record for this book
is available from the British Library

Papers used by Random House UK Limited
are natural, recyclable products made from wood grown in
sustainable forests. The manufacturing processes conform to
the environmental regulations of the country of origin

ISBN 0 7126 7940 5

Typeset by MATS, Southend-on-Sea, Essex
Printed and bound in the United Kingdom by
Mackays of Chatham PLC, Chatham, Kent

Contents

Dedication

To all my friends around the world – I give them my inside view on how things can work inside some football clubs

Acknowledgements

Of course the first person I should like to thank is Harry Harris, British Sports Journalist of the Year 1998 and Chief Football Writer of the *Mirror*, for helping me to write this autobiography.

I'm also very grateful to Estelle and to my children for their support; to all my fans, not just at Chelsea but around the country and the world (and I mustn't forget all the ladies at Stamford Bridge who worked very hard for the club); and to all the players and coaches with and under whom I have played during what I think is a colourful career.

Then I must pay tribute to my advisers and friends at First Artist Corporation; to Nicki who looks after my diary and to Jon and Phil Smith.

I also have in my thoughts my golfing partner Jimmy Creed, my big friend Mr C. J. Carlos, Mr Santini of Santini's restaurant and all the staff at the Scallini's restaurant in Walton Street. They have always been very good to me at San Lorenzo's too. And Lance who has taken care of everything to do with Ruud Wear.

Finally my thanks to all those people that have helped me while I have been in England, especially all those lovely fans.

Foreword

I began writing my autobiography at the start of the 1997/8 season, not from the moment I got the sack at Chelsea. I've been writing down my thoughts about my life for a long time now and, as I review my notes, one thing has struck me as very curious, if not incredible: a pattern seems to repeat itself, time and time again.

Relaxing and reflecting on times of trouble, I came to the conclusion that feelings at the time of an upsetting departure from a club can not only heal over the years, you can actually change your perspective about events and your emotions towards them. There have been times in the past when I have felt tricked and used, yet years later I have returned to these clubs to be honoured, in sharp contrast to the acrimonious clouds under which I left. How curious, then, as I wrote about my leaving Feyenoord, PSV Eindhoven and AC Milan, that events at Stamford Bridge were shortly about to mirror my past.

My career spans many years in different countries and at different clubs, so this book contains many triumphs and many lows and, of course, my innermost thoughts about my sudden exit from Stamford Bridge. At the moment I still have a bitter taste in my mouth about what happened to me at Chelsea, but you can tell those involved that they can say whatever they like about it because I know, and they know, that the fans have their own opinions and are asking their own questions and won't be fooled. Even when I returned to Amsterdam in the days after my sacking a lot of English people stopped to talk to me in the street, and they all seemed to understand about hidden agendas. It's impossible to dupe them, they are too intelligent and worldly-wise.

Yet, I have learnt a valuable lesson for the future about how I would do the job differently when I return to football. The bitterness and anger at my sacking lasted less than a week. Once that disappeared, everything was easy for me, because now I don't have to cover up the truth.

1
THE BOY FROM THE JORDAAN

Sometimes I go back to the streets where I was born on 1 September 1962, and where, as a little boy, I played football. Rozen Dwars Straat, where I grew up, was in the Jordaan district of Amsterdam. 'Jordaan' is a Dutch version of the French for 'garden' – 'jardin' – and this was a very special sector of the capital. All the streets were decorated with different kinds of flowers, and the narrowness of those streets meant they were full of perfume and colour. Colour didn't seem to be anything out of the ordinary in the Jordaan. There wasn't much space to play football, but the kids would still kick around anything they could find, in a similar way to the fabled players of England and other countries who first developed their skills in the streets. It was in the confines of Rozen Dwars Straat that I first kicked a ball.

My family lived in one split-level room on the top floor of

a three-storey apartment block, and this was my home for the first ten years of my life. I had a very happy childhood. The neighbourhood was renowned for its friendliness, cosiness and open-mindedness. Nobody ever closed their curtains, not even on the ground floor. It was open house for everybody, and people came and went, dropping in on each other all the time. Because it was so open and friendly, no one had anything to hide – as we would say in Holland, everything was straight in your face. There was great community spirit, you felt part of one big family and the happy atmosphere your surroundings created. You were proud to be Jordaanese. I always try to go back to those streets whenever I can. They're humming with students these days – perhaps they gravitated to the area because of its intimate atmosphere. It is still the heart of the city and the students have ensured the area retains its vibrancy.

It is a good thing that the Jordaan had this special ambience for I was an only child. My mother was an only child too, my grandpa had only one sister, my father's family lived in Surinam, so there were as a consequence very few relatives around. I used to hate Christmas because there was just nothing to do. Memories of Christmas as a young boy are of listening to the Philharmonic Orchestra on the radio and spending the whole day indoors trying to occupy myself, watching films like *Scrooge*. The big day was the fifth of December – St Nicholas's Day – so that was the day I looked forward to because that's when presents were handed out.

I suppose I was introduced to football when my father gave me a ball and took me to the local park, and it was in the Jordaan that I experienced my first real challenge in the game. I wasn't quite nine years of age when I became a member of a clubhouse. On Wednesday afternoons we'd play football, and at other times we concentrated on our studies or spent time on creative expression, or, as kids like to do, watched films – usually on a Sunday. You went to the clubhouse whenever you felt like it, paying a small fee on your arrival. There was plenty of space for the smaller children as well with climbing frames, sandpits and the like provided for them, but I and my friends spent most of the time playing football.

The clubhouse organised a summer camp every year, and we used to spend five to ten days at the Putten camp and meet up with other kids from other clubhouses. I suppose its *raison d'être* was as a break for overstressed parents, but it was great fun for us. There was a swimming pool there, the camp was close to a forest, and there were plenty of varied activities. Every summer we played a football match against the rival clubhouse from Rotterdam. It might have been just a small summer camp for kids, but the rivalry was fierce – we played as if it were Ajax of Amsterdam against Feyenoord of Rotterdam. An extra competitive edge was added by the donation of a cup; a ball of silver foil it may have been, but to us it was a glittering prize. It might as well have been the European Cup, it meant so much. We marked out a big pitch and the people from nearby villages would gather around to watch. I can't really remember much about the games, and I don't think I ever scored, but what I can recall is the excitement the match generated and the enthusiasm of the spectators. It was something I'll never forget for the rest of my life. It was from that moment I understood precisely the passion and drama of playing football on a proper pitch. I've still got the clubhouse team photo. I've no idea where any of my team-mates might be now or what they've done with their lives, but certainly none of them plays football for a living.

The clubhouse stands out in my early memories, but among my earliest recollections I suppose the strongest feelings are reserved for my grandpa on my mother's side, with whom I had a very special relationship. I loved that guy.

He was a really big man, tall with big feet, about seventy years of age. His name was Martinus, but we called him Tinus. He was a plumber by trade, and he was crazy about organs. I remember going with him a couple of times to Utrecht on the train to visit organ exhibitions. I wasn't too interested in this musical instrument, but it was a joy to be with him, to see him smiling and happy. I spent a great deal of time with Tinus because he really made a big impression on me – he was such a sweet man, and a lucky one too. I've never met a guy so lucky at cards. He *always* won. For some reason my mother couldn't handle that, but that just made Tinus laugh. He had lost his wife early on and he brought up my mother all by himself. I remember making a drawing of him one day while he was asleep, quite a good one. Sometimes he could get very angry with me, but all I had to say was 'Sorry, grandpa!' and he'd forgive me. He had known hard times, but he never lost his capacity for a big smile. I like to think I take after him in this way.

I never knew my grandfather on my father's side, he died very early. I can only recall seeing him once, and then only when he was very sick. He had come to Holland from Surinam, a former Dutch colony on the coast of north-eastern South America. My father, George Gullit, taught economics at the Kweek School voor de Handel in Amsterdam, but I never went to that school. I didn't want to; you know how teachers are – they can be so strict, and doubly so when their own kids are in the classroom, so I felt it was wiser to go to another school. He was born in Surinam and had played football there as a young man for the national side, and for top league teams Sonny Boys and Transvaal; when he came to Holland to attend university he also played on an amateur basis for Real Sranang. My father told me he had a phenomenal shot and that during his playing days he loved to be tough, committing himself to hard tackles that would make his opponent fly through the air. He had massive calves – they used to call him 'Devil's calves' in Surinam. The tackle that propelled the unfortunate man on the receiving end through the air was known as a 'bokkoe'. My father would fly in and block the ball with his studs, forcing his opponent up and over.

He loved to do it, but on one occasion it got him into deep trouble. My father's father was at the time the headmaster of a Christian school, and once, when my father played for Surinam against British Guyana, he executed a couple of these famous 'bokkoes', and his father got to know about it via the newspapers. One paper labelled my father a pig because he kicked so hard, and when my grandfather read it he chastised his son for bringing disgrace upon the Gullit name. Well, at least that's how my father tells the story. He says his father went mad and almost threw him out of the house, he was so ashamed of him.

My mother's name is Ria Dil. She worked as a cleaner at the Rijksmuseum in Amsterdam, starting work horribly early at seven in the morning. The Rijksmuseum is a lovely old building full of the exquisite works of Dutch masters like Rembrandt and Rubens, and I got to know it intimately. I knew every inch of its underground tunnels – which really just served as short-cuts for the staff – and it was so exciting exploring them. But it wasn't just these passageways that fascinated me; from an early age art held me in its grip, and it still does. There was one painting in particular – *Nachtwacht* (*The Night Watch*) by Rembrandt – which I loved to go and look at, and the 'icons' – religious paintings in a sort of wooden cabinet whose two doors you open – in the museum had an immense effect on me; each of them told a story in graphic detail. It was marvellous just to stand there, look at them and try to understand the imagination of the painter, how he captured these historical moments and his

15

interpretation of them.

One icon in particular always stands out in my memory, a scene just after the execution of John the Baptist at the request of Salome, Herod's daughter. It was a shock when I first saw his severed head on that gold plate. The horror and cruelty of it all was expertly captured by the artist, and its three-dimensional effect made it so clear, so alive, a work of genius. It was as if the subjects were real, they almost offered to step off the painting. I remember very clearly being rooted to the spot in front of it for ages, staring at it intently. I would get very close to its surface, and I can still recall my amazement that it was actually composed of real paint!

It's a culture in Holland to visit museums and galleries. Between the ages of about ten and fourteen art appreciation became part of my schoolwork, and in addition to visiting my mother's place of work I would go to the Van Gogh museum and also to the Stedelijk museum where there was this amazing picture entitled *Who's Afraid of the Red, Yellow and Blue?*

Art for me was fascination and confusion in equal measure; sometimes it was difficult to understand and many people would engage in heated debates over the meanings of certain paintings. Sometimes it tipped over into violence and people scratched them with knives or defaced them in other ways simply because they didn't agree with what they saw as its message. The *Nachtwacht* was attacked with a knife at some stage, and my favourite *Who's Afraid of the Red, Yellow and Blue?* was damaged about three years ago. When it was taken to be repaired there was huge controversy over the way it was restored. The painting basically consisted of three wide stripes of red, yellow and blue and had been meticulously painted with tiny little dots. Allegedly, during the restoration someone painted it with a roller, as a decorator might do. It caused a major row between the insurance company and the restorers. I suppose some might see the humorous side of that, but so many take their art very seriously.

There's such a wide variety of movements in art that it can be a bit difficult to follow at times, but there was always one artist that enthralled me more than any other: the Dutchman M. C. Escher. A mathematical, scientific type of artist, his drawings are full of brilliant illusions and paradoxes. There's a famous one I loved to gaze at – *Ascending and Descending* – in which you can follow the figures and trace their steps going down stairs, only to come to a point above where they originally started. In another you can trace the passage of water coming in a downward direction through a series of floors, yet it ends up on the same floor or above it.

It was the mystery, the almost paranormal nature, of those compositions that attracted me, but then I've always been fascinated by the unknown. From an early age I've wondered about space and time and whether we are the only beings in the universe. I have read many books about this, and one in particular made an impression on me: Erich von Daniken's *Were the Gods Cosmonauts?* As a result of reading that book I took an interest in the Nazca plateaus in Peru where, from the sky, you can see an amazing array of strange, geometric patterns on the desert floor, and of course you are left wondering how this could have happened when ancient civilisations knew nothing about flight. One of my great regrets in life was Holland failing to qualify for the 1986 World Cup in Mexico as I had planned to visit the many mystical Aztec sites in that country, and I've promised myself one day to fulfil that dream. I still read books about the Mayans in Peru, Ancient Egypt and other lost cultures. My love of books began very early, and I haven't lost it.

I enjoyed my schooldays. When she left for work my mother would take me to grandpa's, and I would sleep for an hour in bed before school started. It wasn't long before I switched schools to one a little further away from home, the J. J. van Noord School in Amsterdam, I suppose because my mother had attended it and wanted me to go too.

The schoolyard was a bit bigger there and I was able to play football with the other boys during breaktime, even though there were too many kids for the space. We played with anything. There was a temptingly large parking area which divided us from another school for older boys between the ages of eighteen and twenty, and we would all jump the fence to go and play there. Someone would find a brick which was then placed on its end to serve as a 'goal', in a similar manner to the way we used the basketball post at the clubhouse; the object of the game was to 'score' by striking the brick with the ball and knock it down. We played our version of football every single day. The standard was high and the milkman's son, who was much older than us, used to join in.

The next stage in my football development was moving home at the age of ten to a district called Amsterdam Old West, and in this neighbourhood there was a big recreation area called Bilbao Square, a space especially created for kids, on the concrete of which was marked out a football pitch fifty metres by thirty metres. I never played on the main pitch; we preferred the adjacent basketball court where the target for a 'goal', the post of a basketball net, wasn't so big, and no one had to stay there and guard it. Because the court area was so much tighter, and the goal so much smaller, it was imperative to develop your skills and technique, to be quick-thinking rather than chase the ball all the time. The football was so good that a nice guy of thirty who we called Uncle Jan used to join in.

It was here that I first kicked a ball in the company of Frank Rijkaard, who also lived in the district. Frank was one of my close friends. We went to the movies together with all our other friends, but football was our passion. We squeezed out every last moment playing there, carrying on right up until my mother's shouts of 'Rudi, you have to eat!' filled my ears. Then I'd hide where she couldn't find me in the hope she'd think I wasn't there. I'd carry on playing until it was dark, until I was almost the last one left.

I suppose it's a striking coincidence that two future international footballers should have met by chance as kids playing street football in an ordinary city square, becoming such close friends in the process. We didn't go to the same school, but we caught the same number seven tram which ran from my house to the school, and when we were both eleven years old we just seemed to spend for ever standing on that platform, waiting. As kids do with their lack of inhibition, we just got talking. When I got home after breaking the ice for the first time, I told my dad about Frank and he just said to me, 'Yeah, I know his father very well – we played football together in the same team.'

As a result of our meeting and talks on the tram, we ended up playing football together hour after hour on Bilbao Square. But it was always difficult to get Frank out of bed on a Saturday morning – he would sometimes sleep until one o'clock. I wouldn't say I didn't like my sleep on a Saturday, but ten or eleven o'clock was enough. Frank's mother was always delighted to see me and would greet me with 'Ruud! I'm glad you're here, go up and get him out of his bed.'

Looking back, all our friends who joined us on the square had talent and it never ceases to amaze me that only Frank and myself went all the way to the top in football. Some lost interest, others' lives ended in tragic circumstances. One of them was Jerry Haatrecht, my best friend. On 7 July 1989 he was among the 185 passengers on board a Surinam Airways DC-8 which crashed at Zanderij airport in Surinam, leaving only fifteen survivors. Included in the death roll were many players in a team from the Dutch Premier League formed by black players with Surinamese roots, some of whom I had played with on the square. For most of them it was their first visit to their native country. I was not personally invited to take part in the tour because of my Serie A commitments, although I know they would have loved me to go. AC Milan couldn't release me and I spent the summer in Italy. I was in the gym in Milan when Frank came to break the news to me. 'Do you know the plane has had an accident?' he said. I couldn't believe it. The tragedy of the crash had a great impact in the Netherlands at the time, and it was certainly one of the lowest episodes of my life.

Sometimes I have the feeling that Jerry's still here. We were very close, both of us playing for the same amateur and club teams. He was such a kind person, and when he gave up playing football he earned his living selling goods in the marketplace. Many people came to his funeral, all the relatives and friends of everyone who died in the crash. I made a speech at the funeral, but I couldn't finish it for the tears rolling down my cheeks. It took me a long time to get it all out of my system. Jerry wasn't the only friend I lost – many of the team died, including a lovely guy called Percy with whom I used to go out so often when Feyenoord toured Indonesia in pre-season. It's still incredible to think that Jerry and Percy are no longer with me. Sometimes it's very hard, and both will always be in my heart.

I remember after the crash relatives of one of the survivors, a small boy, were trying to coax him back on to a plane to overcome his understandable fear of flying. He said he would only do it if he could come to Milan to watch his favourite Dutch players. The club was delighted to invite him over for the final of the Italian Super Cup between Milan and Sampdoria that year – and we won the game too.

I was only about eight years old when I played for my first amateur football team, Meerboys near the Ajax stadium, the club my father had played for before me. In the early days it was simply a case of joining in with the other boys at the lowest level. Unfortunately my time with Meerboys was relatively short-lived for the family moved to Amsterdam West and it was just too far to travel. It was a nightmare journey for me, about forty-five minutes by tram. Luckily I was making progress and I was able to move on to a higher grade of amateur football with a club called DWS Amsterdam, based near where we lived. Back in the 1960s it was a professional team that had made it all the way to the top division, and even now it's a well-recognised name in Dutch football. It has since merged with Blauw Wit, the club for which Frank Rijkaard used to play.

There was a completely different environment to the cosy world of the Jordaan on the west side of Amsterdam, and it was difficult at first to adjust, but I did have a friend of mine also playing for DWS and together we were selected to play for Amsterdam Youth – quite an honour at the age of twelve. One of the privileges of making the grade with the team was the opportunity to train and play at Ajax with the best players of my age group. What amazed me was how cocky the other players were in their behaviour, even in their running style. They all strutted around, looking so flashy. It took me aback, but I was attracted to it at the same time: the way they held themselves said to the entire world, 'I am an Ajax player.' Although I never wanted to be quite as smug as that, it certainly demonstrated to me that there were many levels of power and prestige in football life. I don't know that it did them much good – nobody in that particular group came through to play the professional game at the highest level.

Although I didn't really know anything about tactics, positional play or the theories of the game, I was chosen to play for the DWS first team in the sixteen to eighteen age group, which was a big promotion for me and a great honour. To be perfectly honest, I was very interested in football and loved to play it, but wasn't yet engrossed with its intensities and complexities to the extent that I thought I could make a career out of it. I was just enjoying it, relishing it, even desiring it. I never had an idol – Pele, Cruyff or Beckenbauer – like most kids of my age, and I never became a fan of any one club; I suppose my immense interest in the game itself overrode any tendency towards a particular team. Most kids had their bedroom walls plastered with posters and photographs of their heroes; I've read how Dennis Bergkamp used to have pictures of Glenn Hoddle and the Spurs team on his. I had only one on mine, a glossy photo of Hans Krankl, the Austrian captain. I honestly didn't know who he was, but I thought he had a kindly face so I put him on my wall.

I rarely went to a game – watching it didn't have the same attraction for me. The first game I ever went to see was a European Cup Final between Anderlecht and Hamburg at the Olympic Stadium in Amsterdam. I went with all my friends, including Frank, but, do you know, I don't even remember the result of the match! It was just a thrill to be in that magnificent stadium, to be part of the electric, magical atmosphere. The biggest thrill of all was gaining admittance without paying anything – well, not much. The turnstile operators saw us coming and we held up our hands so that it looked as if we had fistfuls of money. They were full, of course, but only with small pennies, which we plonked down on the counter before moving off sharply. It didn't add up to very much, but by the time the operators realised, we were in the stadium, and I don't think they cared very much either way.

As a result of my promotion at DWS, for the first time I tasted success and felt a sense of achievement. I often wonder, why me? I wasn't very skilful, I didn't have many tricks, but I was determined to learn. I suppose I stood out in more ways than one so far as the selectors were concerned. I was always big for my age, and when I played competitive football that didn't always make me popular with the opposition. I remember one game when I was taking a free kick, which I loved to do, and the opposing team had constructed a defensive wall, as usual. In situations like this I always employed the same tactic: fire the ball hard and straight at the players. I used to put so much power into the shot that the next time I took a free kick nobody wanted to be in the wall. The first time I did it I had a group of mothers shouting at me from the touchline. 'You can't do that!' they screamed, and the next time I took a free kick they were telling their sons not to stand in front of it! You can imagine how that ball must have felt slapping into your body at a rate of knots on a really cold winter's day.

It always seemed cold to me whenever we played, and I always looked forward to a nice hot chocolate or cup of tea at half- or full-time. You know, there is a myth about English footballers that they are the only ones that play in the cold in short sleeves, and that continental players can't handle it. It isn't true, but still it doesn't make sense to me when I see youngsters in England training in freezing weather wearing only a pair of shorts and a skimpy top. All those red legs! I'm in favour of gloves, hats, anything you can think of to make time spent on the training ground as comfortable as possible.

A year after my debut with DWS I persuaded Frank Rijkaard to go for a place on the team. I talked to him at great length about how much I was enjoying it and how much he would enjoy it too. 'You have to come with us, Frank,' I pleaded, and he did. So for the first time we played together in the same side. In fact there were many friends from the Bilbao Square days in that DWS team – it gave us a great feeling of unity, and there was good team spirit.

Amsterdam Youth played regularly against other city youth sides, and eventually I was selected for the National Youth team. I now had to travel to Utrecht, about twenty-five miles away, every Wednesday after school. I hated it. We were reimbursed for travel expenses, but it was the hassle of the trip and all the bus and train switches that got me down. It was always at its worst when it rained. We all know how flat and windy Holland is, and I used to get drenched, my jeans soaked right through. I didn't want to be dependent on my parents for a ride; I was always brought up to take on responsibility and do things for myself. My father had a car but never once offered to take me, though he was usually busy teaching and couldn't get away. Sometimes I was clever and managed to wangle a lift with my friend's parents, but most of the time I either cycled or braved the bus and the train.

When I did get a lift I always felt a twinge of guilt, remembering my father's words: 'If you want to do it, do it yourself.' Of course he was pleased for me and my good progress on the football field – he was a footballer himself, after all – and what he really meant by those words was, if you want something badly enough in life you should go for it but not rely on other people. He always stressed the importance of self-reliance, and about once a week I was left at home alone in the evening to fend and cook for myself – and before you think it was anything fancy, it was usually chips with mayonnaise. (I'm sure I'm going to get a lot of stick for this in view of the proper dietary requirements of a young professional footballer these days, but I don't care, so long as I don't get stuck with the tag 'Mr Chips'.) My father's philosophy I can now appreciate was the right one, it has made me the man I am today.

Despite being proud of my achievements, my father wanted me to concentrate a bit more on my studies and succeed at school. I really tried hard, but my bad memory fought against me (even though later in life it was a boon because it retained the details of fewer problems!). I was not very good academically, but I could remember a handful of mathematics formulas which I would write down furiously on a piece of paper the moment an examination started. I always recall it as a huge relief when I'd done that successfully – I saw mathematics as an elaborate and giant maze, and the formulas were the maps I could use to navigate my way around. I was, though, good at languages – I just seemed to have a feel for them. Now, having played my football in various countries, I can speak four: Dutch, German, Italian and English. I was not all that hot at the grammar side of things, but even when I was very young I could understand parts of conversations in other languages.

I firmly believe that everyone has a talent in life, and by the time I was thirteen I was beginning seriously to convince myself that mine lay outside on the playing field. Trial games for the National Youth teams were always the most interesting, the most tense and the most fascinating because you constantly wondered how you had performed and whether you would get into the team. The successful players were always informed by letter, and waiting for its arrival was another small form of torture. When I was thirteen I was selected to play for the twelve to fourteen age group. Also in that squad was Erwin Koeman, brother of Ronald, both of them graduating through the ranks to international status with myself and Frank. We were never in the same starting line-up because I was younger, but after twenty minutes of every game I had to come off the bench and play in the same team as him.

A year later I was captain of that side and Frank was playing alongside me, but a year after that Ger Blok, the National Youth team coach, made the decision to allow me to skip an age group and go straight into the big boys' team, the sixteen- to eighteen-year-olds, where I played under his guidance – and with future stars such as Erwin, Ronald and Frank, Wim Kieft and Johnny van het Schip – for three years. I travelled abroad for the first time when I was chosen to play in a tournament in Poland, the youngest player in the Holland National Youth squad. I remember playing France, and they had a player in their side, Touré, who was the best I'd ever seen. I was amazed by the range of his skills and the quality of his technique. I've since spoken to Frank Leboeuf about him and he tells me that Touré was a great player for France, but had his problems. He had heard that the French tennis player Yannick Noah had had a hand in helping him. I followed Touré's career – he was three or four years older than me at the time of the tournament – as a midfielder with Nantes, Monaco and France. He was an inspirational figure for me at the time, but I had honestly not yet decided that football would be my life.

During this time I continued to turn out for DWS, and just before I turned fifteen Barry Hughes, the coach at the professional football club Haarlem, approached me and asked me to sign up. Barry was a Welshman who had played with Don Howe and Bobby Robson at West Bromwich Albion, ending his playing days in Holland after marrying the Dutch television celebrity Elles Berger, and then moving on to management. At first my father was against the idea, wanting me to carry on at school – he felt that was far more important. Having been involved himself at a high level in football he knew the pitfalls of the game and the vagaries of making a living out of it, but his opposition wasn't for one moment because he doubted my abilities. Barry Hughes came to our house and spoke to him; my father told him to come back at the same time on the same date next year. There were a number of other scouts sounding out my father at the time, including some from Ajax, but Barry did just as he was told and I ended up at Haarlem.

I trained with the Haarlem first team every day. By that time football, just football, and only football was inside my head twenty-four hours a day. I wanted to play all the time and train all the time, and sure enough, like a snowball rolling down a hill, I gained momentum and grew in stature. Barry was great to me, he was a very kind and helpful man. He was very serious and ambitious about his work, but could also be very funny. He was always taking the mickey out of himself for being bald, and during carnival time in Holland he had his own song which became a hit, and its first line went, 'I have on my head a room-sized carpet'. It was very strange to say the least to see your coach dancing and singing like that on television! Barry always talked about England and had a fund of stories about his playing days, of how he was the great entertainer and the crowd loved him and shouted his name. The way he described it, you just couldn't help rolling about in stitches. He contributed a lot to making my years at Haarlem very happy ones.

As my father feared, involvement with the game at such an intense level began to affect my schoolwork. When I joined Haarlem Barry found me a school there, but it was just too much of a struggle for me to meet both commitments. I used to catch the train from my home in Amsterdam at 7.15, arrive in Haarlem at 7.45, catch the bus to the school and get there by 8.30. Except for Wednesdays, which were rest days, I would leave school at 5.00, catch the bus to the training session at the stadium, then endure the thirty-minute train journey back to Amsterdam. If I was lucky I'd be home by nine to do my homework. Every night I was tired out, and with such a schedule something had to give. At least my teachers were sympathetic, and they always tried to cajole and encourage me. 'Come on, you can do it,' they'd say; 'Come on, Ruud, try it again,' if I got something wrong. Often I did try again, and on occasion I succeeded, and I am very grateful to those teachers for their understanding and their attempts to stimulate my interest in schoolwork, but ultimately it was an impossible task.

2
BIG RUDI DIL

The name on my birth certi-
ficate reads Rudi Dil. There's a story in Holland about how
everyone came to find out about my real name. I was
travelling with the Dutch team in my early days as an
international and one of the journalists spotted my photograph and name in my passport. There was no big deal made
of it, it wasn't big news in Holland or anywhere else because
I was not yet well-known as Ruud Gullit. In fact it's proved
very useful, particularly when I've been travelling or booking
into hotels, and in the photograph I have a completely
different hairstyle. Everybody knew at Chelsea because all
the promotional photographs that were sent out when I
signed had the name 'Dil' on them. I have no idea why that
was the case – I didn't ask them to do it and I wasn't
consulted about it – but whenever I've signed a contract I
used Rudi Dil, because that's my name.

I decided to change my name to Gullit when I was at
DWS, about the time when I thought I'd probably be a
footballer. I just didn't think Rudi Dil sounded like a

professional soccer player, so I asked my father if I could use his name. Everyone in the Jordaan and at school still knew me as Dil, but to the country and the world at large I was Gullit. It can be bizarre when I go to passport control and I'm recognised by customs officials, then they read my passport and wonder what's going on. They're convinced I'm the famous football player, but it doesn't say so on my official documents.

I suppose I could change my name officially to Gullit, but there's a reason why I won't: I'm the last of the Dil family. I was convinced there weren't any Dils left, but only recently I was travelling with KLM and a Dutch air hostess came over to me and said, 'I'm a Dil too – there can't be many of us left,' and she wondered whether we were related in some way. I don't have a big family and I didn't think there was any connection, and anyway she came from another part of Holland.

It's strange how names mean different things in different countries. I had a friend in Holland who was called Ronnie Pinas, a word which has no significance in Dutch. If there was someone with that name in England, though, you can just imagine the reaction. Dil is very close to Bill in sound, and that *does* mean something in Dutch – arse – and I didn't really want to be known for the rest of my career as 'The Bum'. Dil was also an easy target for the comedians because of its namesake herb, and in Holland they used to call me 'Crocca', after the Dutch word for crocodile. I am very proud of my name, but, as I've said, Gullit suited a Dutch football player much better.

My name's not the only thing I've changed either, and I suppose some reading this will want to know the origins of my 'dreads'. When I was at Haarlem I had a wet perm because at that time they were in fashion, and my mother loved it. But it took them four hours at the hairdresser's to get it into shape, to get the big curls instead of the small ones, and the skin on the top of my head was red raw with minor burns – it was very painful. It then reached the stage where I got bored with it, even though it was still very trendy, and because I loved reggae music so much I decided on dreadlocks. So I twirled my hair for hours on end for two years until it transformed itself. It's fascinating looking back at all those old photos to see how much my appearance changed. From then on people just got used to the dreadlocks, and I gradually became associated with them.

Then, at some time during my fourth season in Milan, I shaved off the moustache I'd had since the age of sixteen. I remember the day well – I was just in some sort of funny mood, and there I was in the dressing room having a shave. Frank Rijkaard also had a moustache at the time, and I turned to my friend to show him what I'd done, and he just laughed. It took everyone several days to get used to it. Such a small thing, a moustache, but such a big change when it's gone!

About a year after the World Cup in 1990, I went through another big appearance change. One day I marched into a barber's shop and told him I wanted a new look, a shorter style. I brought with me a magazine picture of a guy who played with one of my favourite American reggae bands and told him to copy it. I could sense the barber thinking, Oh no, this guy appears on the telly nearly every day, if I screw it up my name will be mud. He started by shaving the back of my head, and after the first attempt it looked like a tasselled lampshade, and in a curious way I resembled an Ancient Egyptian pharaoh. I told him to have another go and take off everything under the dreadlocks. He took off one layer, I didn't like it; he took off another, still not satisfied; then he took the whole lot off and for the first time in years I could feel the skin on the back of my neck. I had the look I wanted, which is the way I look now.

I'm sure some people change for the sake of fashion or because of peer pressure, but I have changed – whether it be my name or my hairstyle – for myself, not anybody else. I just want to be able to look in the mirror in the morning and say, 'Hey, I'm happy to be me – I'm happy to be here.'

I first discovered girls at about the age of twelve. In those early days it was nothing serious, more playing at being adults than anything else, kissing girls and bragging about it afterwards, telling your friends at school, 'Oh, didn't you know I kissed her?' They would eagerly reply 'No!' and want to know more, and I made sure I exaggerated every tiny detail.

I had my first more serious relationship when I was fifteen, and the memory of it is still vivid. After a while this girl, whose name I won't make public, began to talk about engagement, but I was not so keen. I was far too young, and I suppose women are more mature at an earlier age than men and attach far more importance to teenage love. By the time I was sixteen, though, I had become very shy and embarrassed with girls as the result of what I suppose is a common experience. I went on holiday to Benidorm in Spain with a group of friends. We all trooped off to the discothèque and, as boys do, began to ask the girls to dance. I went up to one girl and delivered the politest of requests, but she refused – and, worse still, danced the very same song with another guy. It was my first experience of rejection and, away from home, it was hard to take.

Never mind: when I got back to Holland I threw myself into football once more. On Sunday, 19 August 1979, thirteen days short of my seventeenth birthday, I made my professional debut as centre-half for FC Haarlem, the youngest player ever to kick a ball in top-level Dutch football. I thought I came through my first match pretty well. A year later and I had left the defence behind for the position of central striker, and in that second season I scored fourteen goals, Haarlem were crowned champions of the Second Division, and I was voted Player of the Year for that division by my fellow professionals, winning my first trophy – the Silver Boot.

It was during the 1980/1 season that English club scouts began to take an interest in me. I knew next to nothing about it at the time, but I have since been told that the manager of Arsenal, Terry Neill, and Don Howe (with whom Barry Hughes had played at West Brom) came over to Holland to watch me perform. Barry encouraged this, describing me to them as 'the Dutch Duncan Edwards'. The asking price was £200,000, but because Haarlem were struggling financially I am told Barry was prepared to go down to £80,000.

In my third season with the club, Haarlem finished fourth in the First Division and qualified for Europe, but I was not to be part of the team competing in the UEFA Cup because in April 1982, at the age of nineteen, I signed a three-year contract with Feyenoord, the Rotterdam club paying £300,000 for my services. My European debut would have to wait until an ill-fated trip to Scotland a year later.

Wherever I have gone in my footballing career – whether it be Meerboys to DWS, Haarlem to Feyenoord, Eindhoven to Milan or Sampdoria to Chelsea – every step was a challenge eagerly to be seized upon. I never knew what was waiting for me down the line and that, for me, was the thrill of the move, not the money or the prestige, although of course I was ambitious as a footballer. Often it was a case, deep down, of not really wanting to move; I have always felt an abiding sense of loyalty to the clubs I have played with. But the challenge aspect is always the best one from which to view a move because invariably that brings out something better in yourself.

I was still very young and naive when I joined Feyenoord, but I was made to feel very welcome. The stadium, in terms of atmosphere, was one of the best in the world – the fans make it so – and in 1984 I won my first major trophy when the club finished top of the table, a wonderful moment in my career. Also in that championship-winning side was one of the world's all-time greats, Johan Cruyff, who had moved to Feyenoord for one season before his retirement. Cruyff, so long associated with Ajax of Amsterdam, caused a major stir when he packed his bags and headed off to Rotterdam. I suppose there he could exact some measure of revenge on Ajax by proving to them he was still strong enough to play top-flight football, after the club's doubts over his fitness and potential adverse influence on the rest of the team during his last days there.

I was totally unperturbed about any influence he might exercise over us at Feyenoord – I was just delighted to be playing with him. As a young player, who could wish to be learning from anyone other than the master himself? In fact I was privileged to work with two of the biggest names from the great 1974 World Cup squad, for Wim van Hanegem was also at Feyenoord. He had just retired as a player and was assistant manager of the club. He trained us every day, a marvellous man to work with, and he became one of the most important people in my life at that time, more so because I could turn to him if I wanted to chat or talk about other issues. I kept in touch with him when I moved on, and our relationship is still good.

Van Hanegem and Cruyff were in their mid-thirties, experienced men of the world who'd seen everything there was to see in the jungle of professional football, and the advice they lavished on me is something I will never forget, words which still ring true today. The most important thing, they told me, was that when I got to their age I should be able

36

to look back on my career with pride and feel sure that I exploited my potential to the full; don't look back, they would insist, and think, If only I had done this or that. I'll never forget one particular nugget of wisdom from Wim: 'Sometimes, Ruud, remember that being even an average but competent player is preferable to being at the peak. When you are average you can be kicked out of any club anywhere, but you will find eight or nine clubs waiting to give you a job because nobody seems to get bothered about those players below the top level. There is no in-fighting when you arrive and no recriminations when you leave, yet you always end up playing for good teams and earning sufficient money without any hostility or pressure being directed at you. If you are one of the big players, one of the top names in world football, you get nothing but trouble.' I was still a naive kid at Feyenoord when I first heard this advice, and I didn't really have a clue what Wim was going on about. I thought it couldn't really be like that, maybe he'd just had a bad time himself. I wanted to get to the top, to be the best, and this guy I respected was telling me I was headed for nothing but trouble. Now I am in my mid-thirties, and I often think, Yes Wim, my friend, you were right by the way.

I also had a very long conversation with Cruyff on the same topic. The club was on a post-season tour in Indonesia, and one day I bumped into him as he was getting out of a lift and we just started chatting for hours in the corridor. Like van Hanegem, he was eager to warn me about what might lie ahead for such a young boy as myself. I was open-mouthed at the fact that such a revered name in world football was taking such time and trouble to give me advice. He told me about the time he left Ajax for Barcelona, of all the hostility and anger that surrounded his departure. He told me about the terrible things that happened to him and his family, the sort of threats he had to endure. Again, it was next to impossible at the time to take all that on board.

Throughout my career I've always wanted to leave clubs on good terms, but sometimes, as Cruyff predicted, it has not been possible. Really, football is no different to most things in life: when you arrive somewhere people are really welcoming and excited at the novelty or prospect of working with you; when things don't go so well people naturally change in their attitude and life suddenly becomes more complicated. But I've always found, and this is a comforting thought for me, that although people can be fickle the club itself stands as a rock, an entity that lives on in its own right, and in that sense it's perfectly easy for me to retain my affection for the club.

Of course I understand how people who are in charge of the day-to-day management of a football club demand success, need it, and so do the fans, but I think everyone – spectators, owners, directors, managers and players – has to derive pleasure from the experience through the good and bad years. Unfortunately, although this sounds strange, the more successful a club gets the less joy people get out of it, for to strive for success is an all-consuming and exhausting process – I've experienced it and it's difficult to fight against the anxiety and irrationality that results. The more successful a club is, the harder you have to work to maintain a standard, and it becomes a momentous task actually to try to improve. It's no longer simply the innocent hope of that first breakthrough and the sheer joy at its arrival; expectations soar and the fear of failure grows more acute.

I've seen this everywhere I've been in football because all the clubs I've joined have in some way been struggling for recognition, prestige, silverware or a return to glory days of the past – that's the challenge that drives me, rather than going to a club already in the highest echelons. It's why I went to Chelsea on a free transfer. To achieve success means hard work and putting together a talented squad, and at first it is a thrill to see an underachieving club that has won little in its past becoming big, its name feared, the desire to win all the time implanting itself. What has irritated me in the past, though, is to see that club then turn hard, introverted, too self-critical shortly afterwards, simply because success has squeezed out the love of playing football as a game. It is then that the atmosphere turns sour and players become numbers instead of human beings.

The reason everyone has so many expectations of us at Chelsea was not only because we had won the FA Cup – that was in my first season as player coach anyway, when acceptance levels for standards were lower – it was more because of the energetic and attractive brand of football we played and the calibre of players I brought in for 1997/8. Some of our big wins were completed in such an exhilarating style, with such panache, that it lifted people too high. A month or so of middling results and everyone starts to panic. The most important thing to remember when you first get that elusive success is to keep both feet firmly on the ground; the worst thing that can happen is to let it sweep all consideration aside.

Of course, it is always special to go back to play against one of your former clubs, and it's amazing how attitudes can change again. When I moved from Feyenoord to PSV Eindhoven, for instance, with all the ramifications of that decision, I expected a hostile reception when I returned to Rotterdam wearing the PSV strip – sure enough, the crowd threw bananas at me. Yet when I went back again recently the club was marvellous, and honoured me by making me a life member.

Some football clubs have always had, and probably always will have, hard and determined people at the helm, and perhaps that is the only way to run one. A player is respected and cosseted when he performs a job for them, but as soon as form dips the question marks go up and there is no hesitation to sell when an offer comes along. In contrast, when a player feels he has done as much as he can at a club and wants to seek fresh challenges or benefit himself by moving up the ladder or to a more demanding arena, he can be accused of being a selfish bastard and a deserter. It's unfortunate, but it is true that clubs want it both ways.

Jurgen Klinsmann's position at Tottenham was a perfect example of that. Jurgen is a personal friend of mine, and I have every sympathy for a player of his stature in the game wanting to determine his own future. Jurgen did very well for Spurs in the 1994/5 season, but because he was given the opportunity to play for Bayern Munich – the biggest club in his home country, the one he supported as a boy and the one closest to his heart, and who would turn down an offer like that? – and he wanted to leave I can imagine some people thought less highly of him. One moment he was worshipped for all he was giving to the club, the next he's letting everyone down. The question here, and for any other player in the same situation, is whether or not he has the right to do it. If it was in his contract that he could leave after one season, then no one can criticise him for taking up that option. The Bosman ruling has altered the balance of power to a large degree and has made clubs rethink their strategies; now it seems to them that players have too much say over their own destinies. That's why players are now offered seven-year contracts – ten years in the case of Ronaldo at Inter Milan – because a club knows that players can achieve a phenomenal transfer value. Even an average player can be sold for five million these days.

Bosman's case has rightly changed the face of football. Players can no longer be treated like slaves, they have to have the rights they enjoy as citizens of a democratic country outside football. But what Bosman had to go through to achieve this end was scandalous. Football authorities left him completely out in the cold, and as a consequence he lost everything: his wife, his living and all of his money on legal costs. He couldn't play football for a long, long time. Why couldn't his club have helped him, treated him in a more humane way? Instead they pushed him all the way to the courts, and a fracas that was detrimental to the game's reputation resulted when it could so easily have been avoided. The Bosman ruling is fantastic for players coming to the end of their contracts, giving them much more financial bargaining power, but I wonder if it will be good for the game in the long run. In reality, the ruling favours only a handful of players at the very top end who can take full advantage of it. (Incidentally, there is a misapprehension that I took advantage of the ruling when I came to England, but that is not the case – I was always a free transfer player and my arrival pre-dated the ruling anyway.)

I'll always be grateful to both Johan Cruyff and Wim van Hanegem for taking so much trouble at such an early stage in my career to explain that the road ahead would not always be paved with good intentions. But although I asked them plenty of questions and listened intently to their responses, my head was really in the clouds. Feyenoord was my first big club and it felt like a dream come true. My thoughts at that time were about whether I could actually play to a good standard at this level and maintain it; the future described by these legendary Dutchmen seemed a long way away and out of focus.

Now I can dispense some advice of my own, tell younger players about the pitfalls of football life and how normal rules don't usually apply. First and foremost my message always emphasises the fact that every player must be grateful to be part of football, to realise what the game can give you, the money you can earn from it and the sense of achievement you can have. In the same way they have to get to know the darker side – the harsh words, the backstabbing, the anxiety. Above all else I tell players there is always scope for improvement through determination, inner strength, a certain willingness and good character; if those attributes are always to the fore, the game will be good to you.

The words of Wim van Hanegem and Johan Cruyff always came back to swirl around my head at critical moments in my career, because no matter how big a part I played in bringing glory to clubs when I was there, leaving was always a nightmare.

It was awful when I left Feyenoord for PSV Eindhoven in 1985; despite everything I had done for the club, the crowd gave me a hard time. Naturally the fans didn't want me to leave and they branded me a 'wolf', which in Holland signifies that you are hungry for money, but the truth was I just wanted to better myself. After I announced my decision to leave at the end of the season, some of the fans threw bananas onto the pitch and screamed at me every time I played. They had forgotten that during my time at the club the team had won the League and Cup double.

The situation was no different at the end of my days with PSV. Again I had helped the team to win the championship – even though I had played as a sweeper I had scored twenty-four goals. The season after that we were well on course again, but halfway through that season speculation that a club in Italy might want to secure my services became public knowledge, and in addition there were already existing problems within the squad. It wasn't a question of poor results or indeed anything that was happening on the pitch as such, these were problems about the direction in which the club was going, they occurred in the confines of the dressing room, and were of such a sensitive nature that I declined to go into detail then, and I won't now.

People suspected I was just using these problems as an excuse to get away from PSV, but I was captain of the team and I fully recognised my responsibility to do something about the internal unrest. Players were continually going to the press to air their version of events, and that was driving a wedge between different groups of players, damaging further the harmony of the team. I had to do something, so I demanded that nobody else went to the press and that as captain all comments regarding the club's situation would come from me. I had big shoulders, and I didn't mind if the fans got on my back – I was willing to take the flak for the team. Eventually it came to a showdown and the coach said, 'Either I go or Gullit goes.' There was a board meeting, and the coach was on his way. I felt I got the blame. I was a sitting target, and the directors were so worried about things you could sense they would have been happy for me to take the rap – they certainly, as far as I was aware, made no effort to persuade anybody that the disastrous goings-on weren't my fault. They knew all about the problems the team had because they interviewed each player individually, and their decision was made on that basis. I took the punishment of a large fine – the board's gesture for the fans – but that was just cosmetic and the painful truth lay hidden.

Predictably, it wasn't long before the same carping started up again. There was a debate about my future with PSV mixed in with speculation about Milan's interest in me, and the directors insisted they didn't want to sell me. The crisis escalated and once again I ended up looking like the bad guy, the deserter, and the club did little to deny the rumours. At the end of that last season at PSV it got so bad I was being barracked during the warm-up. As club captain I normally led the team out, but no longer: the team went out first and fifteen seconds later I followed them onto the pitch to be greeted by a cacophony of booing. But again, I was happy to deflect the hostility away from my team. I'm not sure whether the rest of the players really understood what was going on, but by this stage of my career I knew precisely what was happening. I carried on playing in the matches, and the adverse reaction from the fans simply spurred me on to greater efforts. I felt I could only justify myself by turning in a good performance, and that is what I did. I played my heart out for PSV during those dark days.

But something had to give, and eventually, after a training session one day, I was called into the Philips offices. To my utter amazement Silvio Berlusconi, the president and owner of AC Milan, was sitting there. I had absolutely no idea he was coming over, but there he was talking to PSV representatives about taking me back to Milan. He had offered seventeen million guilders, then a world record £5.5 million. It was a relief as much as anything to find that the persistent rumours had some substance to them; up to that time it had all been hearsay, newspaper gossip and endless speculation. I had a chance to go to one of the most prestigious clubs in Europe. The deal was struck.

But before I left I was determined to help PSV win a second championship. In the crucial match away from home against VVV Venlo I played as well as I could and scored a goal, but it was still a frightening experience for me. I remember in the early stages of the game I was attacking the Venlo goal and I clearly heard someone in the crowd behind the goal shout, 'After the game I'm going to get you!' PSV won the match, we clinched the title, I scored the goal, I did everything I could. At the end of the game the fans rushed onto the pitch to celebrate, and you've never seen me sprint so fast to get to the stairs and the safety of the locker room.

We still had one game left to play, at home to FC Den Haag, and even in the same breath as the crowd celebrated the team's title win they booed my name. As usual, this only spurred me on to greater deeds, and I scored two goals. Then, a strange thing happened: the fans started to applaud me. I was surprised, but it was a pleasant surprise. It meant they had begun to realise how committed I was to PSV's cause, but at the same time that I was ambitious, that not too many players get the chance to play for AC Milan, and that my leaving did not reflect the fact that PSV was no longer important to me.

Despite the rancour surrounding my departures from Feyenoord and PSV, I have happy memories of my time at these clubs, and those memories are far more important to me than a condensed version of what went wrong. I insist on thinking about the good times and putting the bad ones into perspective. If we're honest about the way football clubs are run and the way footballers think about themselves and each other, there can only be one conclusion: things will rarely run smoothly when so many diverse characters are thrown together into such a small world. There are certain aspects of life inside the dressing room which may seem at the time to be fraught with difficulties, but when you look back on it two or three years later you can be more relaxed about it – sometimes I was right, sometimes I was wrong. I never have any regrets, even when at times the full facts of these problems emerge at a later date. As far as I'm concerned that's for others to wrestle with their consciences over.

All I can say is that I did whatever I had to do with the best intentions and never for purely selfish reasons. Of course I was interested in my welfare as a footballer and acted accordingly, but, as captain at PSV, I acted on behalf of my team first. It fills me with great sadness when I read the 'revelatory' autobiographies of famous footballers or managers who have in a fit of pique indulged themselves in all manner of criticisms and accusations. This is not my style. A footballer owes his career to the whole gamut of experiences he goes through. I make mistakes, everybody makes them, but the important thing is to give people both inside and outside football the space to repair rifts and rectify errors. Little or nothing is ever achieved by a public execution.

3

THE MILAN YEARS

So in the summer of 1987, after PSV had seen out the Dutch season so successfully, I made my way to Italy. Milan was like a different world when I arrived there – everything was new to me. I didn't speak the language for the first three months, and I found it very difficult to settle. I did one or two things in those early days that I now look back on and think, Rudi, how could you do anything like that? For instance, I'd only been in Italy about three months when I agreed to sing live in front of a three-thousand-strong capacity crowd with my band, Revelation Time.

As a teenager I craved to be part of a real reggae band, and during my playing days in Holland I liked nothing better than to listen to Revelation Time playing either in concerts or cosy little nightclubs where the atmosphere was fantastic, the sound was good and everybody was relaxed. I then met the band members one day in a cellar at their digs when they were rehearsing, and they asked me to join in. Now, the truth is I can't sing and I can't play bass guitar – even though I've tried hard to – but still I picked up the instrument and plucked away, and it felt good to be part of it. Our association progressed to the extent that we cut a record together – 'South Africa' – even though I only had one line to sing. Then I made a record on my own and really got the opportunity to test my voice, though the worst part of it all was appearing on the Dutch equivalent of *Top of the Pops* and doing all those 'play backs' where you mime to the record, just standing there looking like a complete idiot with your mouth going silently up and down. I hated it – and I didn't like the song much either.

Although I felt ridiculous miming on stage, I always thought I wouldn't mind singing it for real in front of an audience. I knew I couldn't sing but I didn't mind having a go. But still, as I've said, when I think back to that concert in Milan – what in heaven's name was I doing? I have to apologise for that concert! What made it worse, I had already come to a decision that the band didn't deserve to be in the shadow of my celebrity, especially as I was by far the least musically talented person there. I wanted disc jockeys to play Revelation Time's records because they were good songs, not because of their association with me. So I called it a day. One thing did make me proud: the band composed and recorded a song especially for me called 'Captain Dread', and I liked it a lot.

I was fascinated by Italy, and Rome in particular. I remember once after a friendly match against Lazio my friend Marco van Basten and I decided to go for a nice little walk around the city. We did the usual things a couple of guys would do: found a bar, ordered cappuccinos, talked to the people we met there and just had a good time. Even though our Italian was still very rusty, the bartender was used to dealing with tourists and had no problem serving us.

Afterwards we were walking through the streets back to

our hotel when by chance we bumped into the club's general manager, Paolo Taveggia. When he saw us he went out of his mind.

'Ruud, Marco, what on earth are you doing here?'

He was literally jumping up and down, we thought he was going to have a fit. We explained to him that we had been having a stroll through the city and had enjoyed ourselves – we thought there was nothing wrong about that.

'You can't do that in Italy!' he screamed. For some reason he just couldn't believe what we were telling him. 'This is Italy, not Amsterdam!'

'But we didn't do anything apart from chat to a few people. It was nice.'

'No, no, no, you can't do that!'

We didn't know whether to laugh or not, we thought he might be having us on. We thought it couldn't really be that bad; after a game in Holland we used to go out with friends and could often be found in the company of people from the media. We explained this to him, but it only made him worse. By this stage we thought he was going to have a heart attack, he was so red in the face. Every time we tried to calm him down he just got angrier. He told us that the press in Italy were constantly on your back so the last thing we should be doing is walking around town courting discovery and disaster. I began to wonder what I'd let myself in for. I remember hoping it wouldn't be like a prison in Milan. I enjoy travelling, experiencing different places and meeting people, but before I'd barely had a chance to do it in Italy's historic capital city, it was out of bounds.

My first press conference after my arrival in Italy centred on this question of media attention. I was asked, 'Has somebody told you how the Italian press will treat you?' Well yes, of course, but I thought the intensity and relentlessness of it must be some sort of exaggeration. So, I was just honest

51

in my response when I said, 'Yeah, I've been told I can't say everything I might want to and it's best to keep things to yourself. I've been told it's wiser to be a little bit careful.' I was shortly to learn my first lesson.

After the conference had finished, I was strolling through the corridors of the Milan offices on whose walls were hung pictures of famous people connected with the club. I stopped to look at Gianni Rivera's, and alongside him in the picture were two policemen wearing identical hats, like the ones you might see in London. I enquired of a journalist who was with me, 'Where was this picture taken?' and the next day in the newspapers that same journalist wrote 'Ruud Gullit didn't even know who Gianni Rivera was.' I was astonished, it just wasn't true. Just because I'd asked that question, a pressman concluded that I knew nothing about one of Italy's most famous footballing sons. I can't escape the conclusion that I'd upset someone with my remarks during the press conference, and that from then on I was the object of their vengeance. I didn't really care what they had written about me anyway, because it wasn't true, but the deceit of it upset me.

After a while, when I'd got to know the journalists and they had got to know me, this story came up and we laughed about it. It is certainly true about the Italian press, though. There are three major daily sports newspapers – *Gazzetta dello Sport, Corriere dello Sport* and *Tutto Sport* – and each sends seven journalists to every training session. The competition is fierce and the intrusion can be overwhelming, but I wouldn't describe it as hounding – they're just doing their job. Perhaps I had the right attitude by giving them my time as much as I could, so when it became tiresome and I said no, they'd give me some space. Still, I've got to be honest: no matter how much co-operation I gave them it didn't stop them from slaughtering me publicly every now and then – but then again they paid me some great compliments too.

I can't really say with hand on heart that the media in Italy is a great deal worse than any other country; wherever there is a passion for sport there is a special interest in reporting it. I've had my fair share of criticism, but generally it is outweighed by more positive aspects. I've always had good relationships with the media in whichever country I've played, but there is little doubt that the word 'intense' was made to describe the Italians and no one else, and there is *no* doubt that this puts additional pressure on the players and managers. If you are not in the team they want to know why, and a non-selected player will sometimes moan to the press and his frustrations will be misinterpreted and conveyed to the readers as something else. But, taking everything into consideration, I feel Italian press reaction is fair because it is predictable: you are good if you play well and rubbish if you don't. We had a code at Milan: we didn't speak about anything, and then it was easier to stay out of harm's way.

AC Milan is a big club – much bigger now than it was in 1986 when Silvio Berlusconi came to the rescue. Sometimes people forget that the club was nearly bankrupt then. When I joined Milan were in the process of building a team that could win everything in the game, and it was probably the strongest side I ever played for. I was worried a little about my ability to get used to the Italian way on the football pitch, because it was so different to the Dutch (and English) way. In Holland the overriding philosophy is to try to resolve everything in a tactical and technical way, with the emphasis on attack – no long balls, play it from back to front. In England the strongest desire is to get the ball forward into the box where you have the opportunity to do maximum damage to your opponents; there's not so much passing, it's all about getting behind defenders. The demand in the English game is for goalkeepers who can kick or throw the ball a long distance, for full-backs who can hit the ball into the channels, and big, strong strikers who can look after themselves in front of goal. In Italy they approach the game in a defensive frame of mind, sitting back and counter-attacking quickly, which can make the game slow and more tactical. Because of the nature of the game in Italy, I used to spend a lot of time during training practising my free kicks using cardboard cut-out walls. You don't get many chances to have a pop at a static defence in Italy, and every dead-ball situation is vital.

But everything is now changing. A lot of coaches in England are looking for more of a passing game, and it's proving very effective because the attitude of getting the ball and the players into the box is still there. Italians are also changing a bit towards more attack, although defence is still central to their mentality. The Dutch are working on a new 'survival spirit' based around huge, solid centre-halves like the six-foot-four-inch Jaap Stam, so that when the going gets tough Holland has tough players to cope.

Despite my apprehensions, I settled quickly into the football routine and began to enjoy every minute of my first season with Milan. One of the most peculiar aspects I had to get used to was hotel life. If we played at home we would stay at the Milanello training ground where every player had a room of his own; if we played away we would leave the day before the match and stay in a hotel. Every time I got home I used to unpack my bag and get my stuff ready for the next game, but I didn't really mind because it's good to concentrate on your job properly.

Mr Berlusconi regularly visited our training complex at Milanello, and these occasions were always something special. I'll never forget the first time I saw him arrive, it was just so stunning. It was the first day of our pre-season training and he flew in by helicopter, landing right in the middle of the pitch. We all stood there open-mouthed. I couldn't imagine the chairman of Ajax or Feyenoord making an entrance in such style – it just would never be accepted in Holland as a normal thing to do. Such ostentation would send out completely the wrong messages, but in Italy it was acceptable – in fact, desirable.

Berlusconi was a charismatic character with many varied business interests, a very determined man with AC Milan in his heart. He did everything in his power to make Milan great, but what impressed me most was his presence. He used to come into the dressing room before matches and give us a pep talk. He always wanted us to represent the club in the proper way, but he never interfered with team selection or tactics, he left that to the professionals. Let me give you an example. Three weeks before the 1989 European Cup Final against Steaua Bucharest he called all the players to a meeting at his house, and we all sat around a big table. Berlusconi made a long, impassioned speech – the final was so important to him, it was crucial to win it. He said, 'Can you do me a very big favour? I know it's three weeks until the match, but can I ask you all when you go to bed not to have sex – I want you all to be like hungry lions before you go into this battle.' Well, I piped up, 'How can you expect me to run well with full testicles?' There have been many stories about disagreements between us, as there have been rumours about arguments with virtually everyone else, but I spoke with him personally a few times and always found him very open. I owe him a great deal.

In those days I was very fit and would run for fun. I was at the peak of my physical powers as a professional footballer, scoring goals, creating them, and generally happy about my level of performance. But it didn't look as though I was going to make the first team at that first training camp. For four days we did non-stop running – it was crazy. I couldn't cope, and was amazed that anybody could, but when I looked around me all the top names in Italian foot-ball, people like Angelo Colombo and Roberto Donadoni, were as fast as anything I'd ever seen. After three days of this madness I'd lost five kilos and I felt terrible. I was totally drained. I went to see the club doctor, Rudi Tavanna, and I told him straight: 'I can't do all this running at the same pace as the others, I'm not built for it.'

When I arrived at Milan I weighed eighty-nine kilos and they had never come across a player of such bulk. They thought I was fat and too heavy. No one had ever made such a suggestion before in my career and I was taken aback. I had always been perfectly fit, and don't forget I am not built like Zola! As far as I was concerned I had a minimal fat percentage in terms of my body weight – in fact, I didn't think I had an ounce of fat on me. But the more I ran the skinnier I looked and the weaker I felt. I was coming to a full stop.

Tavanna ran some cardiograph tests to ensure that my heartbeat was normal for my size and weight, told me to wear a watch which monitored my heartbeat and instructed me to run only between certain bands of heart rate. That meant I had to run more slowly than the others during training, but after just one day I made a full recovery. Over time I found I could match my team-mates for stamina, and the club came to understand that my optimum weight was in fact around eighty-nine kilos. When you come to a new club you want to show yourself off in training and make an impression – the last thing you want to be is sick on the sidelines. Once I had built up my energy levels I was ready to go. I wasn't fat, and when I started playing I proved it.

My position at first in the Milan team was on the right wing with van Basten in the middle and the Sardinian Pietro Virdis on the left. I played for Holland in midfield, but I didn't disagree with where the manager, Arrigo Sacchi, wanted to play me, I never complained. Sacchi did try me as a midfielder, but his opinion was I was better as a forward. People have been discussing for years my best position, but nobody has yet asked me what I think. In fact, I don't mind where I play so long as I'm not messed about. I don't want to be playing in one position one week and another the next. If I'm shifted every time the team has a run of bad scores, which is what happened at Eindhoven, I get irritable. When van Basten injured his ankle and put himself out for most of the remaining season, we switched from a 4–3–3 formation to a 4–4–2, and I just clicked up front with Virdis.

Everything went right that season. We won at Juventus for the first time in fourteen years, which pleased Berlusconi no end (he made a speech before the game, pleading with us to win), and beat Verona 1–0, and from that day we all had a feeling we would win the championship. We didn't lose many games and the fans went crazy. When we went to Naples two games before the end of the season we were a point behind them, and with Diego Maradona in their team and the fervent passion of their fans, it was always going to be a big match, but I really had no idea what a game between AC Milan and Napoli actually entailed. I was intrigued when the club hired two planes instead of one to take us to Naples. It turned out one was for our food and drink.

When we arrived at the airport our team bus, surrounded by police, was waiting for us by the runway, and the players emerged from the plane to be ushered straight on. On police advice the bus was sent back into the city by a different route. As we rode through the harbour area there wasn't a soul around, but when we came to the last phase of the journey to the hotel there was suddenly a sea of people, all of them screaming at us. Purely by chance I caught sight of a little old lady, who must have been nearly eighty, shouting and waving her stick in the air; she'd obviously heard the police sirens, seen the bus and got caught up in the antagonistic atmosphere. As I watched her, she turned to face us and made the most obscene gesture possible. Only the way the Italians can do it. Unfortunately most of the crowd was more mobile than this woman, and about two thousand of them chased us on scooters and in cars, spitting at the bus and generally hurling abuse.

When we arrived the Milan entourage, including the players, was sectioned off from the rest of the guests on the twenty-fifth floor of the Jolly Hotel, but it wasn't a very jolly stay. There were huge barriers erected in front of the hotel, a massive fence to keep the baying crowd away. The minute we stepped inside the hotel we could sense the incredible atmosphere.

Dinner was prepared by Berlusconi's personal chef and none of the hotel staff or waiters was given permission to go anywhere near it. The food was brought out of the kitchens surrounded by Berlusconi's personal bodyguards, and they never stopped watching over us, accompanying us in the lift and spending the entire night walking up and down our corridors. Quite clearly the club was terrified that someone would put something in the food that would affect our performance in the game. I didn't think for one minute our opposition would be party to something like that on the eve of a critical match, but Milan wanted to ensure that nobody came down with a bit of diarrhoea or something. Needless to say, no one was sick.

The Napoli fans' sole mission that night was to keep us awake, but there was no chance of that because we were so high up. Somehow a number of them managed to get onto the floor above us and made some noise, but it wasn't long before I went to sleep. I've always been a good sleeper.

Next day and the match that would decide the championship brought even more scenes worthy of a film script. We were shuttled out of the hotel and onto the coach, and again thousands followed us to the stadium on their scooters chucking stones, tomatoes, oranges, anything they could find. I don't know about the others, but the fans didn't frighten me. I just laughed at them. For me it was an amazing day of entertainment. As the coach pulled up outside the stadium, a fresh batch of Napoli fans hurled more stones, spittle and abuse. You should have seen the state of that coach.

As you might expect after all this fuss, it turned out to be an incredible match. Virdis scored first for us, but two minutes before the end of the first half the referee awarded Napoli a free kick, though it didn't look like a foul to us. Maradona curled it right round me. It was a sensational shot: I was jumping as high as I could to block it and I'm not exactly a little fellow, but it just whizzed past me and hit the back of the net. We were all very disappointed as we trudged back to the dressing room for half-time.

Throughout this half I had been man-marked. This guy – whose name I cannot recall – was just all over me, aggressive, relentless. Even when we were awarded a corner and the ball was picked up and thrown to the corner flag, this defender had a good hold of my shirt. I'd never experienced anything like it – even when the ball was out of play! I was still mastering the language at this stage, but I made my point and I'm sure he understood it: 'Hey, don't you think you're a little bit too early?'

'I do what I like,' he responded ominously.

Virdis looked at me and I at him, and I just began to laugh.

'You taking the piss out of me?' he said, even more ominously.

'Look,' I said in his face, 'I'm far too good for you, you've got no chance of getting me.' And again, I laughed.

He went berserk. You could see it in his eyes. He thought I'd been taking the mickey, and I could see he was pumped up with thoughts of revenge and that he was out to kick me – hard. I knew it was coming, and I waited for the tackle. Even for a big guy I managed to move pretty quickly when it came – although he still caught me slightly – and you could tell his intent from the height he was off the ground. He got the yellow card he deserved. I knew he couldn't risk being sent off now, so I smiled at him and said, 'I now have you in my pocket.'

Finally, given a little freedom – albeit just a little – I managed to produce a movement on the right and a cross for Virdis, who put Milan back into the lead. After his long lay-off, van Basten came on late in the game and again I managed to produce an assist for him, and we were 3–1 ahead. There was no catching us now, the championship was ours, although they did score one more goal.

I'll never forget the images of the last minutes of that game. Napoli had won a corner and Sacchi wanted to make absolutely sure there was no miraculous comeback. Everyone had piled back into the penalty area except Marco van Basten, who stood in attack all on his own. Sacchi's eyes were virtually popping out of his head; he was going completely berserk, shouting at Marco to get back. But the memory that will live with me for ever was the way the Napoli crowd applauded the Milan team after the final whistle. It was a fantastic gesture.

At the end of that season I was voted Best Foreign Player in Serie A, but I've always believed the team is far more important than any of its members, so the most precious award of all that season was definitely the championship, AC Milan's first title for a decade. There couldn't possibly have been a more high-profile club game anywhere in the world than that Napoli match; the worldwide TV audience must have been colossal, and it was great to have shared the experience with a player as talented as Marco van Basten. It was the first season I'd played alongside him, and I know it is often said I was instrumental in his arrival at Milan – and later in that of Frank Rijkaard – but I was never involved in transfers. The best thing about having Marco in your team is that nothing in the world can put him off his game. He has phenomenal mental strength; no matter how much people criticised him, he never got worked up. I think that is great, to be able to shrug your shoulders and get on with life. He was one of the best strikers the world has ever seen, a man with a natural scoring instinct; he could do things on one square yard of grass another player couldn't even dream of. There was never any jealousy between us. We both liked to win trophies, including personal ones like European and World Player of the Year awards, but if I won it he was happy for me, and if he won it I was happy for him.

I've got to say my first season with Milan was the easiest one because there were no great standards to be maintained, no high expectations to fulfil; the squad was just able to say 'Let's go for it!' In that first season I played in twenty-nine out of thirty-four Serie A games and scored nine goals; in my second season I played twenty-eight and scored eleven, although in that year Milan were very much focused on the European Cup campaign. We had some incredible games, particularly against Red Star Belgrade and Werder Bremen. Against the Germans we scored a perfectly good goal – the ball had crossed the line by a good foot – but the Portuguese referee missed it and we went back to the San Siro with a goalless draw. There we won 1–0 with a penalty.

The climax of the 1988/9 season came in the European Cup Final against Steaua Bucharest in Barcelona's Nou Camp stadium. But there was serious doubt over my availability because five weeks earlier, in the semi-final against Real Madrid which we won 5–0, I'd been carried off with cartilage damage that needed surgery. In the first half I had cut inside from the left and attempted a shot on goal, but I didn't connect properly and my knee went. I went straight to the sideline where it was manipulated back into place, and during the half-time interval it was treated with ice. I did come out for the second half and I scored, but made the mistake of going for another fierce shot on goal, and this time the knee collapsed completely. With the final only a month away I went to Rome for an operation, made a quick recovery and was back playing again within three weeks.

But my problems weren't over. The day before the final I experienced some terrible sciatic nerve twinges that left me with little or no movement in my back. I turned out for training that day, but the pain was unbearable, so much so I could hardly walk. The Bucharest coach was out and about spying on that session and must have gone away convinced I would not make the starting line-up. That afternoon I underwent some intensive treatment, but it wasn't making much of a difference. So I had a session with the club's sports psychologist, Bruno Di Michele, who spelt things out to me right from the start: 'Rudi, it is very important if you want to play that you show the team you want to play.' I understood immediately exactly what he meant by that. I was suffering and showing it instead of hiding it – there was no pretence, I was just walking around with a pained expression on my face – and Bruno made the valid point that such an attitude, even though genuine, would give my team-mates no confidence in me at all. They wouldn't expect me to play, and if I did play they would be worried about me and, therefore, not concentrating on the game and giving it their all. Furthermore, looking injured would give my opponents a psychological boost.

To accomplish my ambition of playing in this European Cup Final at the Nou Camp, first of all I had to get my body into good shape, and that meant intensive physiotherapy. I was strapped up all the way from my legs to my spine with tiny lead balls taped to my body at varying intervals. The object was that during movement these balls would apply pressure to certain points on my body, in the same manner as acupuncture needles, which over time would alleviate and eventually eliminate the sciatic problem. In addition, I was put on a course of anti-inflammatory tablets. To complete my instructions to the letter, I walked around with an expression on my face that put nobody in any doubt as to whether I would play or not, and this did make me feel better. I actually played in that final with those tiny balls taped to my body underneath my shirt.

When I walked onto the pitch I was uplifted yet again by the sight of a huge mass of red and black in the stadium. Because Romania was still under the dictatorship of Nicolae Ceauşescu hardly any Steaua Bucharest fans had been allowed to leave the country. There were 80,000 Milan fans in the Nou Camp that night. I felt such a sense of elation – with backing like that you could climb every mountain. From the moment I stepped onto the turf I had this look on my face which read: 'Here I come, everyone.' I was up for the game, even though all those little balls began to slip and slide and fall off once I started to sweat.

During these big games everyone is so focused that you don't actually remember much of the action. There's so much hysteria during and after these matches: fans screaming, photographers falling over our feet and falling all over themselves. It's only later when you watch the video of the match that everything fits into place. When I look again at the team picture for that night, lined up before the kick-off, you can see in the eyes the intensity of our focus. I remember when I scored the first goal I tapped myself on the breast with an open, flat hand as if to say 'Why me? Why should it be me?' I was just so grateful to have scored the first goal, especially because of my injury. Marco van Basten scored the second, and then we knew the cup was ours. When I scored the third, that was just confirmation, and it was sheer ecstasy.

Marco nabbed a fourth a short time later well and truly to seal the win. I was delighted for him and wanted to celebrate, so I chased after him so that I could hug him and tell him how proud I was. But he kept on running and I kept on running behind him – I thought he'd never stop. All of a sudden, totally without warning, he came to a halt and I almost crashed into him as he fell down. I finally got hold of him after what seemed an eternity; he had actually run halfway around the pitch. When I asked him why, his explanation astounded me. He had seen a Dutch guy before the game who had paid an awful lot of money for one of the advertising boards, and he promised Marco a 'present' if he scored a goal, ran over and posed in front of the board. 'You tight bastard,' I told him. I made it perfectly clear to him that I wasn't happy he had made me run all that way after him just so he could stand in front of an advertising board. I'm sure that this is a true story, but you can never be sure with Marco.

In the fifty-ninth minute I was substituted. The fans applauded me off, appreciating my contribution to Milan's success on the night. I came off with cramp, which is hardly surprising given the amount of time I had been out for my operation and recuperation. However, journalists wrote that I had been taken off because I was suffering from pain in my knee. It just wasn't true, and it angered me at the time; moreover, it cast doubt over the reliability of my fitness, something which would stick to me too closely over the coming years. Nobody asked me why I'd been substituted, and apparently no one had noticed that a couple of minutes

I'm just a 'little midgen' of three at Christmas time at Nursery School

Growing up fast and looking very smart for the family album picture taken in the Rakin district of Amsterdam when I'm six

My first 'team' line-up. At the age of eight at summer camp in Putten

My grandfather Martinus, a big influence on my life

Below: My mother and father, Ria Dil and George Gullit

Making the grade at the age of fourteen in my first National team when we played against Spain. I made it all the way through the ranks with Erwin Koeman (bottom right)

On holiday in Spain at the age of eighteen

Johann Cruyff (above) and Wim van Hanegem (below) were the major influences at the start of my elevation to top grade football at Feyenoord

Making my presence felt
in the air playing against
Ajax, and showing my
speed – when I was still
young enough – with
PSV Eindhoven against
Utrecht

Showing off one of the trophies we won at PSV Eindhoven with Michel Valke (left), Rene Van de Gijp (right) and Frank Arnesen. Below with Marco van Basten who won the Best Player award

Facing page: I was always closely marked at AC Milan, here by William Kief. However I didn't object to the close attention of owner Berlusconi and my team-mates celebrating championships and European Cup triumphs. Paolo Maldini is sporting the hat and scarf and Giovanni Galli is the gentleman on the right

Rinus Michels is one of the best and most repected coaches I've worked with, so it was a great honour that he presented me with the award for European Footballer of the Year 1989, in Paris

before I came off I had rolled down my socks, a sure sign of the onset of cramp. Nevertheless, I was a happy man as I sat down on the bench because AC Milan had won the European Cup. When I finally got my hands on the cup with the big ears, I had such a pure feeling of joy, something I'd never experienced before. It was ecstasy.

The worst moment on such occasions is when all the photographers crowd round you, demanding your attention. They are always there in such numbers that it's somewhat of an anti-climax for all the loyal fans in the stadium who want to celebrate with you. I was very glad that during the 1994 World Cup in the United States the number of photographers was limited when Brazil were handed the trophy.

That night it was celebration time for the players, a time to let our hair down after all the intensities of our European campaign. You can imagine how long it went on for. The next day the plane took us back to Milan. I was perfectly all right when we boarded the plane, but when I got off the pressure inside the plane during the flight had caused my knee to thicken and it was very sore. Immediately I went to Rudi Tavanna, the club doctor, for an examination. By the time I got there the knee had swollen up completely and was extremely painful. Tavanna got a syringe and sucked out all the liquid from inside, then put me on yet another course of anti-inflammatory drugs.

Unfortunately there was no time to rest. I had to go with the Dutch national team to Finland for a vital World Cup qualifying tie. There was obviously no chance of my starting the match, but the management still wanted me there, even if it was just to sit on the bench. However, the team was performing very badly and it wasn't long before I was being asked to get on the pitch, so I did. I managed to produce a good cross for Wim Kieft who scored the winning goal that ensured Holland would make it to Italia 90.

Another night of celebration. After the game I felt nothing in the knee, there seemed to be no problem at all, so I went out with the boys. Next day it was perfectly normal as well, and I assumed I'd made a miraculous recovery. But on the way back to Milan the same thing happened again: when I got off the plane the knee had thickened up. Again the excess fluid was drained from it, but I needed another operation to resolve the problem within. This time I was able to take a holiday and give my poor knee some rest, but when I returned to Milan for pre-season training the knee swelled every time I went for a run. It was full of water and horribly uncomfortable. My great friend Ted Troost had a look at it and gave me three possibilities for getting it sorted out: a doctor in Sweden, one in the United States, or one in Belgium. It was just instinct that made me choose the latter, and that was when I first visited the sports injury specialist Dr Marc Maertens, who was to save my career on several occasions.

4

TED TROOST

I first met one of the most important men in my life when I was just eighteen years of age. My coach at Haarlem, Hans van Doorneveld, suggested I go to see Ted to see if he could help with my recovery from a persistent ankle injury I had sustained which didn't seem to want to go away. When I visited Ted I was in for a big surprise: he just got hold of my ankle, made some movements, and I could hear the ankle joint go 'clunk, clunk, clunk'. The pain was so intense I thought I was going to hit the ceiling – in fact I nearly fainted. But it seemed to do the trick, and after that session with Ted the recovery speeded up.

Ted is a fascinating character. I was drawn towards him not simply by his apparent expertise, but also by some of his ideas. He was not just an accomplished practitioner in physiology, but a kind of sports psychologist as well. He dealt with the mental and physical sides to a sportsman, and in a most unusual way that involved the senses and the mind. He taught me so many things that have helped me not only on the football pitch but also throughout my life.

An example of Ted's unorthodox methods was that he could harness the energy from an atmosphere, whether it be inside a football stadium or a lift. We would sit down together and talk for hours and he would say to me, 'Okay, what happens when you first walk into an elevator?' There are times when you walk into a lift and there are three or four people in there already, and as you walk in, the doors shut behind you and the lift begins to move, you can feel the tension in the air. We've all done it many times, and we've all looked up and watched those numbers lighting up as the lift ascends or descends because nobody wants any eye contact, any sort of contact at all. Ted explained to me that it was pointless wasting so much energy through nervous tension like that for absolutely no purpose whatsoever. 'What do you do to break that tension?' he would say. That's easy: just say, 'Hello, everyone. How are we all today?' There'll usually be someone who won't think you're a nutcase and will answer, and when that answer comes you can feel throughout your body the tension being released, and all the occupants become more relaxed as a result.

It's the same when you go, for instance, to a cinema and there's only one arm-rest between two people. The guy next to you might want to take the front part of it, or he might want the back part, and you're left guessing – needlessly expending nervous energy – wondering what he'll do. You can sit through the whole film in a state of complete distraction, once again using up energy for no reason. Instead of concentrating on the film you might scratch your head and then tense up, wondering whether your part of the arm-rest might no longer be there for you. The end result is you've wasted your time going to the cinema. Instead, wouldn't it be simpler just to say, before the film starts, 'Hello, which part of the arm-rest would you like, the back or the front?' You'd resolve the situation immediately and you could get down to watching the film, the very reason you're sitting there anyway.

The same set of rules can be used inside a football stadium. When you're the opposing team and you walk into a stadium for the first time you can sense the atmosphere, whether it's going to be friendly or hostile. You have to analyse what is happening to those players, particularly if they are entering a stadium whose fans are bound to be hostile: as soon as they emerge from the players' tunnel most of them walk onto the pitch with their heads down, and that signifies that they're not sure of themselves, they're lacking confidence and are worried about their surroundings. And that pleases the opposing team's fans.

I'll never forget one particular match – a vital European Cup tie away, Red Star Belgrade against AC Milan, in November 1988. I had a hamstring injury and I couldn't play, but I had tested it out by running in the hotel corridor because I couldn't do the training in the morning. Instead of playing I was sitting in the stands among some 80,000 watching the match. But all of a sudden, to everyone's surprise a really thick fog descended on the stadium and it wasn't long before you couldn't see from one end of the pitch to another. The game had already started, and only by the screams from the other end of the stadium could you tell that Red Star had scored a goal, through Savicevic in the fiftieth minute. It was clear there was only one choice for the referee: play could not be allowed to continue. Play was suspended and the match rescheduled for a second start twenty-four hours later.

The next morning Milan contacted Ted in Rotterdam to see if he might be able to treat my hamstring so that I could play. They sent a private aeroplane to Holland to pick him up and flew him straight to Belgrade. He gave me some treatment, loosening up the hamstring so much that when I ran along the hotel corridor I felt fine. I said to the club, 'I think I can play,' but Ted was most specific when he spoke to the management and insisted that although I could take part in the game it could only be for half an hour or so, otherwise I would probably zip up the hamstring again. As a result of Ted's warning, I was selected for the squad but on the bench for the kick-off.

This time round I walked out onto the pitch with the other players, although I made a point of coming out last. It must have come as a massive shock to everyone in the stadium to see me there when the day before I was in the stands. We were inspecting the pitch, but I did what I always do: stand tall and look up, not down, eyeing the crowd. I turned slowly through three hundred and sixty degrees and looked intently at every section of the stands; I then walked around slowly and fixed my gaze on everyone I could see. The Red Star fans went berserk, whistling, screaming and shouting at me. After five minutes of this, they stopped, and at that moment I knew I was in control of the situation.

It was going to be a tough game, and there was so much at stake it really was an emotional time. It was clear we had scored the first goal, an own goal – the ball had crossed the line by a distance of at least one metre, and I mean one metre – but the defender cleared the ball and the referee didn't allow the goal to stand. It was incredible, I'd never seen anything like it before, and never have since. The ball wasn't just over the line, it was almost touching the back of the net! Nobody could believe the decision and it made the entire Milan team angry. There was already a hostile atmosphere inside that stadium, but now everyone was crazy. Marco van Basten scored first, then Red Star came back with an equaliser through Stojkovic to make it 2–2 on aggregate, and the game was on a knife edge.

We thought it couldn't get any worse, but it did. Roberto

Donadoni had a nasty accident, falling on his head and swallowing his tongue. All the colour drained from his face and he went completely white; no one could look at him he was in such a bad way. The doctors put his tongue back into place and he was stretchered off. That meant I had to come off the bench with only a few minutes of normal time remaining before half-time. As Donadoni was rushed off to hospital the Milan players went back to the dressing room, and everyone was very upset, not only about the disallowed goal but because of the uncertainty of Donadoni's condition. Then we heard an announcement in Italian coming loud and clear over the tannoy: Donadoni was all right. The announcement was greeted by whistling from the crowd, as if they were unhappy that Donadoni was all right and out of danger for his life. Our much respected centre-half Franco Baresi was crying with anger and all the players were so frustrated – we were all determined that Red Star should suffer as a consequence.

Despite the clear warning from Ted, I played not only the whole of the second half but extra-time as well. In the very last minute of extra-time Milan won a free kick by the touchline. I ran into the penalty area and launched myself at the ball to meet it as it sailed over. I was full of determination, but as I rose one of the Red Star defenders brought his knee up and it connected with my thigh. I suffered a bad dead leg and couldn't move for a while. The tie went to penalty kicks, and Milan progressed, winning 4–2.

Afterwards I was curious as to how it had been possible for me to play nearly eighty minutes of high-intensity football on my dodgy leg, when I'd been advised not to. Ted told me that it was because I was able to absorb all the negative vibes in the atmosphere and convert them into positive energy, and for that reason I managed to run around much longer than the forecast thirty minutes. It's a kind of formidable strength, the mental equivalent to the physical reaction of adrenalin pumping through your body, that someone can summon up when they are involved in an accident, for instance: even though someone is trapped under a heavy weight, they are so focused and involved that they can lift almost anything. Such enormous energy is generated by a passionate crowd, and instead of being drained by it a player should utilise it. By losing your head it's impossible to build up that controlled anger that fills you with positive energy.

Ted has also told me to observe how people execute simple actions, like entering a room. Some people can walk into a bar, head held high, and everyone will turn round and have a look. That's because they possess charisma, there's something about that person that attracts without any sort of contact. Others walk into a bar and no one would even notice, and that's because there's something negative about them. You could walk into a room with your eyes closed and still sometimes be more aware of what is in the room when you are focused and concentrated, noting even more perhaps than someone not so focused who walks into the same room with eyes wide open. When you consider how that translates into football terms it's often described as 'vision' – the ability to find your team-mate with a long-range pass without looking up, for example. It means being open to everyone, aware of everyone's position, and having the necessary talent to slot balls quickly into the right channels. It can be as much about a feeling as vision or touch; it can even be related to that sense of tension in the lift, something that you can clearly perceive or feel but you know how to cope with it.

I brought Ted Troost to Chelsea when I was player coach there, and I believe he had a positive effect on the players, helping to guide them in the right direction, to open their eyes and make them aware of all the ways in which the senses they possess can function. I like to think for that reason the players at Chelsea are now more aware of each other, more open, and can understand each other better. Ted came to the club once a week, every week, and he talked to the players. It was an experiment at first; I'd decided that if he wasn't getting any response there would be no harm done and his sessions would be discontinued. But in no time at all Ted built a rapport with them and they quickly learned and appreciated his methods.

I like to think what Ted brings to the game is similar to the experience of driving a car. You don't drive your car as such, you drive all the cars around you. If you see somebody swerving in a car in front of you, you can go right or left to avoid them, but what you are doing is observing the car movements around you and anticipating and reacting to what happens to them. If a football player can adjust his thinking on the pitch to this theme – you're driving everybody else's cars, not just yours – then greater teamwork and improved understanding is bound to result.

Some players are extremely nervous before a game and need to be calmed down; others can be too relaxed and have to be motivated. Every player is different and needs a specialist kind of attention, which Ted provided for us at Chelsea. The players have to work at it, to respond effectively, otherwise the whole exercise is pointless. In the same way it's pointless having a dietician at the club if the players aren't interested in eating anything but fish and chips. It's a question of educating them, making them understand the benefits of such actions, and once that is taken on board then they are self-motivated.

After a while, at Chelsea the players used to come into the kitchen and demand good food; to a great extent they had lost their interest in sausages, chips and burgers. They wanted pasta and fresh vegetables, and if any sauces were integral to the dish they wanted them separately so they could control the amount they ate. When we went to hotels the menu was devised in consultation with the club doctor and the players were particular about what they ate. They knew that if they ate the right foods it would give them extra energy. It got to the stage where I didn't have to chase up on them anymore. Anyone can go home after a match and pig out secretly on the wrong foods, but they were going home and eating the right things. The evidence of the benefits of this kind of lifestyle for a professional footballer was there on the pitch for everyone to see. If a player doesn't have a good sense of responsibility, strong self-motivation and pride in his performance, then I will change him. As Ted has always said, unless a player is in peak mental and physical condition he is not going to perform at an optimum level and he's not going to be worthy of his place in the team. Someone with greater determination and commitment will be – it's as simple as that.

5

FROM MILAN TO SAMPDORIA

Milan had begun its domination of European club football and Silvio Berlusconi's electronic empire was beginning to flourish (he'd even flown in his own television crews and equipment to the Nou Camp for the 1989 European Cup Final because the Spanish technicians had called a strike).

It was a pleasure to be part of that Milan team. They had a different kind of style, a fusion if you like of the Dutch philosophy – all-out tactical attack – and the Italian – sit tight and don't give anything away. The mixture was formidable, and AC Milan were six years ahead of their time.

In December 1989 we made our way to Tokyo and won the World Club Championship, beating South American champions Atletico Nacionale of Colombia with Evani scoring the winner in extra-time. But back home, during my third season in Italy, regrettably things were to turn a little sour. I was often out dealing with the repercussions of my knee injury and managed to start in only two Serie A games, scoring one goal. But again we had a great end to the season, retaining the European Cup in Vienna at the expense of Benfica, and again I made another surprise appearance in a major final. Milan needed extra-time to dispose of KV Mechelen of Belgium in the quarter-final and again against Bayern Munich in the semi. At the time of the final I had only just come back from yet another operation, but Sacchi wanted my presence on the pitch, certain it would have a beneficial psychological effect on the Milan players and a detrimental one on the Portuguese. We won the title of European champions for a second successive time with an angled goal in the sixty-eighth minute from Frank Rijkaard.

The following season, 1990/1, was the first since my arrival in Italy that Milan failed to win any domestic or European silverware, although we had beaten Olympia Asuncion of Paraguay in the World Club Championships in Tokyo. Two goals from Frank and one from Stroppa once again gave us the title of most powerful club in the world, and that compensated to some extent for our coming failures. Also I returned to fitness after my lay-offs the previous season, managing to play thirty-one games.

There was bitter disappointment in the European Cup. We entered the competition in the second round after a bye from the first and were held to a goalless draw at the San Siro by Belgian champions Bruges, fortunately beating them 1–0 in the away leg. At the quarter-final stage it was Bernard Tapie's Olympique Marseille versus Silvio Berlusconi's AC Milan, the clash of the tycoons. In the home leg I scored in front of 83,000 after just fourteen minutes, but Jean-Pierre Papin equalised before half-time and the second half was goalless. We were without the suspended Marco van Basten for both legs, and Marseille were definitely up for the return leg with the tasty prospect of knocking out the reigning European champions in front of a noisy home crowd. It turned out to be one of the most bizarre games I've ever played in.

In front of an ecstatic 38,000 capacity crowd Chris Waddle scored a goal fifteen minutes from time, but a short while later the floodlights failed and plunged the stadium into darkness. The players left the field, and officials at the club managed to get some form of lighting going again. After a long break the Swedish referee ruled that the game had to go ahead, but we refused and stayed in our dressing room. UEFA took strong measures against us, changing the result to a 3–0 win for Marseille and banning AC Milan from taking part in any European Cup competition for one season.

As if that weren't bad enough, at the time there were doubts about my fitness being voiced, and Milan brought in Jean-Pierre Papin and the Croat Zvonimir Boban. When Papin's deal was struck, the Frenchman was supposed to have agreed to sit on the bench as my understudy. Milan now had six foreigners under contract, and there was heated debate as to which of them should be first-team regulars because at that time the three-foreigners-only rule was still in force: a club was allowed to sign up to six foreign players, but the regulations restricted the team to fielding only three at a time; the unlucky three, no matter how much they cost or what their status in the worldwide game was like, had to sit out the match on the bench. There is no reserve team football in Italy, so if you didn't play in Serie A, you didn't play at all.

Fortunately I had the support of Mr Berlusconi, but Arrigo Sacchi had left to take up an appointment as coach to the national team, and I don't think I ever had the support of the new coach Fabio Capello. I was constantly in and out of the side. Sacchi used to talk to me for hours about team tactics and strategy, but I never had the same rapport with

Capello. In the 1992/3 season I was only selected for fifteen matches, scoring seven goals, but by the middle of that season I was already sick with the constant sniping speculation over my fitness. The situation culminated in a straight contest between myself and Papin for selection for the 1993 European Cup Final against Marseille. I wasn't even picked for the bench.

I cannot tell you how disappointed I was, even though I was more or less accustomed by that time to non-inclusion in the Milan side. I remember one bizarre incident in particular. I was packed and ready to travel to an away game one day because the team manager, Mr Ramaconi, hadn't informed me I wasn't in the squad. As I was boarding the team bus, Capello said to me, 'Where are you going?' It was pretty obvious I was getting on the bus to go to the away game with the rest of the players, but there had obviously been a total breakdown in communication. I was angry at the time because I had made a fool of myself. But the worst thing at the time of the European Cup Final snub was the rumours flying around more than ever that I had glass knees, couldn't play two matches in a row and wasn't reliable. Nothing hurt so much as that, because I knew it wasn't true. These stories often appeared in the newspapers, but Milan did nothing on my behalf to dispel the slurs. They certainly didn't encourage them, but neither did they deny them. It became a source of immense embarrassment to me, and I also had to contend with the frustration of my position in the squad: if I wasn't picked for the team, how could I prove I was fit? I loved Milan so much and thought I had helped create something special there, even something unique.

When I arrived at Milan the team hadn't won anything for fourteen years. They were in a desperate state, desperate to win something, and I worked very hard to help them achieve that. Now I felt very bitter that I was being turned away, but, as I've said before, I will never bear any grudges towards the club itself – I could never hate AC Milan. At the same time I was having problems with the Dutch national side as well, but again, I could never hate Holland because of it. It's not the institutions themselves, it's the people at the helm; people come and go, but club and country remain for ever. Some of those people are still in positions of authority or influence, but at some point down the line there will come a time when they won't be there any longer. Milan will always be Milan.

It had been a great experience for me, a wonderful and highly successful time, but by the time Milan lost the European Cup Final 1–0 to Olympique Marseille, my time there was over. There was no point in turning up for training anymore – I wasn't in the team, I wasn't even on the bench – so while the speculation about my future raged on I decided to go off on holiday.

I was being linked with all sorts of clubs at the time – Marseille, Paris Saint Germain, Atletico Madrid, Bayern Munich, Torino, even four Japanese clubs – and everyone seemed to be obsessed with me because I was available on a free transfer (I had asked for one in part as a reward for all the things I had done for Milan, and they agreed to that request – it was a nice gesture). It might have been wonderful publicity for me that so many prestigious clubs were interested in my services, but in reality I was sitting at home and there was nothing on offer – the rumour factory and their glass knees tale had put too many people off. Around Europe pre-season training was about to start, so I said to myself, 'Ruud, you're going to have a long, long vacation.'

I did, however, get a call from Milan to tell me that the chairman of Torino wanted to speak with me, but I told Milan quite plainly that I didn't want to go to Torino so what was the point of talking to him? For some reason Milan were very insistent that I should meet him, so they gave me his telephone number and asked me to ring him, but again I said I was not interested. But the Torino chairman was adamant, he wanted to come and see me, so eventually I told Milan, 'Okay, if he wants to drop by he's more than welcome to come and see me.'

He turned up alone. Yet after he left a huge press contingent, photographers and television crews surrounded my house. I was very angry and surprised because only three people knew that this private meeting was taking place. The publicity may have been good for Torino but it wasn't for me.

To take my mind off the problems surrounding my future in the game, I went off to play a round of golf. I'm often asked these days what I enjoy doing away from the football field, how I relax, even though most people think I'm already relaxed when playing or managing. Of course I'm not relaxed – I'm eager for the team to do well and inside I'm as tense as the next man and very much involved in the game. Laughing a lot is my personal antidote. Football should be fun after all, for spectators and players alike. But away from football I like to play golf.

I have a great deal of fun telling people about my passion for this sport because for some reason they always look surprised. I like the open green fields on a golf course, the opportunity to meditate and chew things over, the chance of a quiet moment all to myself. I don't like playing for points, I like to have a laugh and play for fun. I think nothing of spending hours alone on a golf course, just thinking. It's amazing, the number of ideas that pop into your head; clarity of thought is so vital in all aspects of life. When I was at Chelsea I could be walking along and an idea about tactics or players I should buy might occur to me. My mobile phone might ring and there might even have been a player on the other end of the line wanting to join the club! Often I used just to think about things that had happened in life in general. The golf course is, I find, the only public place where I can totally unwind.

So there I was on the sixth hole, avoiding the Italian press, and I was on fire – I could do nothing wrong. Well, let's be fair, I had had a lot of time for practice recently. Then, my mobile rang. It was Cico Evani, a former team-mate at Milan who had found happiness with his move to Sampdoria.

'Ruud, I am here with the chairman of Sampdoria, he would like to speak to you,' Cico said.

I was gobsmacked, and asked what was going on. Cico replied that the chairman was in a house not five miles away from where I was, and he wanted to see me. Then the man himself came on the line and invited me to his house, and I said yes.

Paolo Mantovani was an amazing man. When I arrived at his home the house was packed with members of his family, and he introduced me to each one. We spoke together for two hours about everything under the sun: about Arizona and how beautiful it was, about the value of being humble, on so many subjects unconnected with football that it was a joy to talk with him and listen to his views. It was some time before he said, 'Let's talk about your contract.' It must have taken less than a minute to discuss terms and conclude our talks, and we never spoke about it again. It was not so much the offer he made as the fact that I already liked and respected the man. From a professional point of view I had something to prove, and that wasn't often the case in my career. After all the misleading reports in the Italian newspapers, everyone thought my knees were permanently dodgy, but Sampdoria gave me the platform to prove to everyone I wasn't finished as a top-class footballer.

The team was a good one: my old friend Cico was there,

experienced men like Mancini, Mannini and Vierchowod, as well as a whole group of promising younger players. The first time I walked into their dressing room I was asked which number I wanted. I've always played in the number ten shirt, but at Sampdoria that was the personal property of a long-standing hero in the team, Mancini. Wearing a shirt with a particular number was not a superstition of mine, because I'm not superstitious, but in Italy and Holland the number ten shirt has great significance: it is worn by the leader of the team, if not the captain, the main figure, and there have been many notable number tens in recent football history, such as Pele, Platini and Maradona. There are also other significant numbers in Dutch football for similar reasons: the number seven recalls players like the great Johan Neeskens; number five is synonymous with Ruud Krol and Franz Beckenbauer; there's Cruyff's number fourteen; and the number eight, always worn by Sjaak Swart, an excellent right winger who is a legend in his home country. But at Sampdoria I asked for the number four because it was the only one I hadn't played in yet. The other players, who knew something about my history of being chopped and changed about the field, laughed at that and it broke the ice immediately. (When I arrived at Chelsea, it was just coincidence that the number four shirt was available – so I gladly took it.)

That season I was on a mission. My first season with Sampdoria, 1993/4, was the equal of my first with AC Milan, the best I'd ever played in my career. I was more relaxed in Genoa than I had been in Milan, mainly because the club wasn't always front-page news. There were times at Milan when I was sick of seeing my name in the papers; sometimes a week wouldn't go by without the word 'Gullit' in a head-line. At the training complex at Milanello there would be at least twenty reporters turning up every day, but at Sampdoria things were more laid back. The night before a game the team stayed the night in a hotel in Nervi, but in contrast to Milan if our wives or girlfriends wanted to pay us a visit then there was no bar.

In my first season with Milan I scored six goals in six weeks, and I did the same for Sampdoria at the beginning of the season – by October I was the leading scorer in Serie A. I'd only been at the club for two months when journalists began to ask me, 'What has happened?' They were no longer discussing my glass knees and how I couldn't perform twice in a row; finally they began to listen to my point of view and I explained to them how I had never made any statement about my injuries while I was at Milan and that all the fuss was pure speculation and rumour. Now, I said, I was playing for my dignity.

There was no more important Serie A game for me than Sampdoria against Milan in the last weekend of October. The week before the match I was asked by every journalist I spoke to if I was intent on revenge. Revenge? No! My mission at Sampdoria was simple: to prove my fitness, help the club to achieve great things, and show everybody I could still play at the highest level. I could never seek revenge against Milan as they had helped me become a true international star, and I still had many good friends at the club. Revenge smacks of meanness and nastiness. I was not vengeful, just out to prove a point.

The game proved conclusively that my knees were not bad. Berlusconi had said a couple of days before the game that maybe he had made a mistake thinking I was past my peak after all those knee operations. And he was taken by surprise by my early-season form with Sampdoria. In the same breath, though, he described me as a 'Milanista' and that his feelings towards me as a person had never changed, even though I wore the shirt of a rival team. I've no doubt he didn't want me to play against his club. The Milan fans, too, were surprised by the fact that I'd played every week for Sampdoria.

After a record-breaking seventy-two weeks at the top of the Serie A table, Milan were knocked off their perch, beaten 3–2 by Sampdoria after leading by two goals at half-time. I scored the winner with a shot about ten or so minutes from the end of the match, and I was deliriously happy about it. At last I had made my point. Not everyone was happy with the fact that I celebrated this goal though: the Milan fans, and even the players, didn't enjoy it very much and felt offended because they interpreted my jubilation as evidence of a mean spirit, a man seeking revenge who has just found the best and most humiliating way to do it. But as I've said, this was far from the truth; they only thought like that because they really didn't know what I had been going through, what a huge weight that goal lifted off my shoulders. In Italy they described my performance that day as one of my greatest ever games. The bigger the occasion, the greater the pressure, the better I play.

But my chief memory of this season was the death and funeral of the club chairman, Paolo Mantovani. He had been sick for some time and spent a long period in hospital. When he died his body was kept in the hospital for a while to allow friends and family to pay their last respects, but although I went to the hospital I didn't want to go to see him – I was afraid of what I might see – but many of the Sampdoria players, past and present, did. I wanted to remember that man as he was the first time I met him when he made such a big impression on me.

The funeral was a very emotional affair, the burial of a man loved by so many people. He was a family man through and through, and he made all his players feel like part of that family. Sampdoria was noted throughout Italy as a family club. There was a massive crowd outside the Catholic church for the mass. Some of the players served as pall-bearers and they carried Mantovani's body into church, and then afterwards for the procession to the cemetery. In front of the pall-bearers was an American band from St Louis, Missouri, an all-black outfit which had come across to Italy especially for the funeral. There were about six members in the band and they played slow, haunting music, so sad, as the coffin was carried through the crowded streets so that all the people could pay their last respects. Then suddenly they broke into lively jazz music. That cheered everybody up and changed the sombre mood completely. It reflected perfectly the way the man had lived his life. There was a clear message played out to everyone present: 'Okay, mourn, yes, but life goes on and I'll always be with you.'

A few days after the funeral Sampdoria had to play a home match against Roma, but it was impossible for us to play with any passion – too many of the players were emotionally drained. Naturally, we lost the match. But Mantovani's legacy lived on, and it demonstrated the new spirit in the team when we went on that season to win the Italian Cup which, of course, was dedicated to the memory of our loved and much respected chairman.

6

HOLLAND – THE GLORY AND THE PAIN

On 1 September 1981 I cele-brated my nineteenth birthday, and I could have wished for no better present than a place in the Dutch national side which played that night against Switzerland in Zurich. I should imagine that few people in football had heard of my name at that stage of my career, but I went on to play international football for thirteen years, winning sixty-three caps in the process, and each time I pulled on that orange shirt I was filled with great pride.

Naturally, my international debut would not have been complete without one of my best friends, Frank Rijkaard, alongside me. We'd started off together playing street football, and here we both were playing for the first time for our beloved country. It was generally a young team playing that day, and as I recall we lost the game 2–1. I made an appearance as a substitute in an attacking role, and five weeks later I played my second game for Holland in Eindhoven's Philips stadium in front of 30,000 orange fans. We beat Greece 1–0 and the coach, Kees Rijvers, said he was pleased with my performance. In fact, he made some lavish predictions about my future in the game.

It wasn't long before Holland were bidding to qualify for the 1984 European Championships in France, but we didn't make a very good start, drawing 1–1 with Iceland in Reykjavik. It meant we needed a good result against the Republic of Ireland in our second match in Rotterdam. At that stage Ireland had a clutch of more than useful players – David O'Leary, Liam Brady, Frank Stapleton and Mark Lawrenson – to call on, and they were favourites in the group along with Spain and Belgium, but we beat them 2–1 and in that match I scored my first international goal. I remember it fondly as one of the proudest moments of my life. After that we played France in Rotterdam and lost 2–1 to the likes of Amoros, Fernandez, Platini, Tigana and Tresor, although after the match Platini praised my performance on the wing.

Almost a year, and five international games, later, on 12 October 1983, we journeyed to Dublin for the return group match with the Republic of Ireland. I was still only twenty-one and playing for Feyenoord at the time, and with 35,000 devoted Irishmen cheering their team on we were two goals down well before the end of the first half, and Liam Brady had scored one of the goals. But we roused ourselves after that. I scored Holland's first goal – which, odd as it may be, I don't remember anything about; it's a funny thing, but the immediate aftermath of a big goal like that is so frenzied and hysterical that your mind literally blots out anything else that happens, even to the extent that you can't recall how you scored – and Marco van Basten equalised with an assist from me. Ireland had been all over us, but we came back spiritedly, working very hard together to save the match. When I scored my second goal, and Holland's third, to clinch the game, I can remember the celebrations. It was a sensational win, and Marco was going crazy, doing handstands and cartwheels all over the pitch. It was also a big turning point in Dutch football because the coach decided to do without some of the older established players like Ruud Krol and rely on the younger players like myself and Marco. It was seen within the country as a big gamble, but we did well and it paid off, and that night was really the moment the 1988 European Championship-winning side was born. From that day Holland went forward with a new generation calling the shots.

After that result I began to feel very much at home in the Holland shirt. We went on to beat Spain 2–1 in Rotterdam, and again I got the winner, but all was to no avail because we failed to reach the finals. Spain had one game left in the group, and had to beat Malta by eleven clear goals to progress at our expense. They won 12–1. We couldn't believe it. I couldn't stay in the house to watch the game so I went out shopping. What's the point of sitting in your living room through all that agony when you can't do anything to affect the result?

The next year Rinus Michels, the coach we called 'The General', took over from Rijvers, and his task was to take us to the 1986 World Cup in Mexico. In our qualifying group were Hungary, Austria, Cyprus and Bulgaria; we finished second and went straight into a two-leg play-off with our neighbours Belgium, losing the first game 0–1 and winning the second 2–1, but going out on the away-goal rule. Our disappointment was immense, our dreams of making it to a major tournament shattered again. It had been a successful year for me on the club front, but the qualifying period for the 1986 World Cup was the only one in which I didn't manage to score. I was sad to see Michels retire as national coach for three months because of heart trouble, but it just goes to show the pressure coaches and managers can be put under. So for that time they assigned Leo Beenhakker. He only lasted three matches – against Cyprus, Austria and Hungary – and I played in all three of them before Michels returned.

Rinus Michels was one of the best coaches in Dutch football and I always had a good relationship with him. He was the man who took Holland to the 1974 World Cup with his famous 'total football' philosophy. By the time of the qualifying stages for the 1988 European Championships in Germany, with such great players as Marco van Basten, Frank Rijkaard and Ronald Koeman at his disposal, the Dutch national team was rejuvenated and we strolled our way in.

Despite losing the first match against Russia, we dominated the tournament. On a personal level I was on a high going into the championships because I'd just won the Serie A title in my first season with AC Milan. I must confess I didn't feel at my peak when the tournament started because I was so exhausted after a long and demanding season, having played in every game of Milan's campaign. I was still doing all right, but I knew I wasn't producing my best form. Marco, on the other hand, was in scintillating form. Every touch of his, it seemed, was perfection itself and I was more than happy to leave the ball for him to do something with.

We beat England brilliantly in Düsseldorf, Marco scoring a hat-trick and me enjoying myself thoroughly on the wing. My most vivid memory of that match is of lining up in the players' tunnel just before going out onto the pitch. The English team came out of their dressing room and we could all hear Tony Adams shouting: 'Come on boys, let's kill these bastards!' Well, we all looked at each other and just had to laugh. You know, the Dutch attitude is a bit less keyed up, a bit more laid back, and we go out there wanting to play attractive football and not really giving a damn about upsetting the opposition or name-calling, so it was a strange moment to experience that type of intensity from the England players. I've never spoken to Adams about it since, but he was only a young lad at the time. England – with the likes of Glenn Hoddle, Gary Lineker, John Barnes and Bryan Robson – had a formidable side in those European Championships, but Marco was in such superb form that they couldn't handle him. It was a great win for us.

But one of the highlights of the tournament was beating Germany in the semi-final on their home ground. It was some party after that game. We went back to our hotel in Hamburg and asked the concierge for the best club in town. While we were partying the night away we had no idea what was happening back home in Holland, where they were dancing in the streets. The German community was extremely upset and stole everybody's bikes! It was a long-standing joke between the two nations, a legacy of the Second World War when the Germans confiscated bicycles because they were a valuable aid to the Resistance movement. As we all know that's the most common form of transport in Holland so it didn't go down too well when some of the German community in Holland stole people's bikes as a joke. However in the end all the bikes were returned and there was one huge festival, but we were oblivious to it all.

By the time we got to Munich we were treating the championship final against Russia as a holiday; as far as the players were concerned, after the defeat of our great rivals Germany we could have gone home happy there and then. In fact, the night before the game we were still in party mood, and we all trooped off to see Whitney Houston in concert.

Even Marco van Basten, who doesn't like dancing at the best of times, was swinging his hips as Whitney gave her all, even though we had been told to stay sitting down in our seats. But how can you not dance to Whitney Houston in full flow? Some might think it a bit reckless to go out and enjoy yourselves the night before a major match, but going to that concert was a therapeutic experience: we were on a high, we worked it out of our system, prevented ourselves from getting bored and ended up in excellent spirits the next day.

Michels treated us to a very special team talk: 'Right guys, as we've reached the final, wouldn't it be terrific to carry on and actually win the cup?' He put it in such an ironic way after the carefree pleasures of the past few days that the message got home, and from that moment on we were focused. Holland had already been beaten by Russia, of course, but we knew we'd outplayed them and that the deciding goal in a 1–0 victory was scored on a quick counter-attacking move.

Up until the final I hadn't been in the greatest shape, but my form and condition quickly improved. My reward was that the coach allowed me to take the free kicks, which he hadn't done up until then. Marco and Ronald Koeman, who had already built himself a reputation as a fast and lethally accurate striker of the dead ball from distance, had both had a go in the tournament, but this was my first turn. So it happened that my first free kick of the 1988 European Championships occurred in the final itself, and I almost placed it in the '7' – the angle between the post and the crossbar – but the Russian goalkeeper made good ground and pulled off a fantastic flying save. However, from the resulting corner I scored a goal with a header, and later Marco added a second.

We were ecstatic, and it was such a great feeling for me, having just become champions with my club as well (but of course there's no comparison: nothing beats winning such a high honour on behalf of your country). I'll always remember rushing over to Rinus Michels, lifting him onto my shoulder and carrying him around the pitch in triumph. As captain of the team, it was my proud duty and privilege to lift that precious trophy for Holland. We were the first Dutch team to win a major tournament, and part of the reason for our success was the camaraderie and spirit within the squad, generated by days on end of living and training together. I regarded the 1988 European Championship win as a reward for what I considered to be an outstanding Dutch side. Again, of course, that night it was party time. I must confess I didn't think it was possible, but it was a better night than our foray to see Whitney Houston the night before. Even the Prince of Holland came.

You are always left with outstanding memories after occasions as joyous as that, and I am no different – the scenes in the stadium after the final whistle will remain with me for ever. I also have a rather unusual incident to recall from the championships. When I left my hotel room to go off to play the Republic of Ireland one evening, I left a small light on and a window open. After the match I returned to my hotel room and it was full of mosquitoes, thousands of them. In a panic I called for help and some hotel staff came up to my room with an industrial hoover, ready for action. But there were so many of them that night I had to sleep in another room.

The next day, some of us a little fuzzy-headed, we flew home. We still hadn't a clue on what scale the reaction to our success had been conducted back in Holland. As we approached the airport we could see tens of thousands of fans, a seething mass of people waiting for us on the tarmac. The plane was asked to perform a fly-over before it landed for the benefit of these fans. It began to bank sharply and manoeuvre in all sorts of directions, and the basic message from the players was 'Just put this damn plane down!' We understood that it was exciting for everyone to have a glimpse of us as we returned to our native land, but we were eager to get off and join in the celebrations. After we'd landed, again we could see thousands of people and a big stage which had been specially erected for our return. When we got onto the bus and began making our way to the capital, the streets were thickly lined from Eindhoven in the south to Amsterdam with screaming, flag-waving fans, who had even managed to infest the entire length of the motorway. The magnitude of our achievement only slowly dawned on us.

When we got to Amsterdam we cruised down the canal in a boat and every single person in the country, it seemed, had come out to greet us and show their appreciation. When we passed by the red light district even the prostitutes in the windows were leaping up and down in celebration and waving to us. It was a strange sight, I must admit: stockings, suspenders and orange bobble hats. Thousands of people who live on canal boats were jumping into the water. It was a crazy day. Everybody was bursting with pride. The finale was to show off the cup in the Museumplein, the big square in Amsterdam opposite the Rijksmuseum. I was honoured by being made a Knight of the Queen, a distinction reserved for the captain and coaches of the victorious squad, but because Michels had already won such an honour, this time he was made a Mayor of the Queen.

It was one of my great regrets that Rinus Michels then decided to step down as national coach. His replacement was Thijs Libregts, under whom Feyenoord had won the Dutch championship in 1984, but at the time he was quoted as having had made some very uncomplimentary remarks about me during an interview for a national newspaper, criticising my work rate and being reported as saying, 'You know what it's like with those blacks, they have that sort of attitude.' My father and I confronted Libregts and wanted to know if he had actually made those comments, and he denied it. You can imagine how I felt about it all at the time. If Libregts thought I was a good player one minute and a lazy one the next, fine, that's his opinion, but, if he had blurted it out publicly it was an extremely unpleasant thing to do. So when in 1988 he was appointed as Holland's new national team coach, again you can imagine what everyone thought I might feel about it.

But everyone was in for a surprise, because I played under Libregts and I played well. I was a professional, and I made a conscious decision to put all negative vibes from the past out of my head. Partly as a result of this, Holland had a brilliant run all the way to the 1990 World Cup Finals in Italy; in fact, we qualified unbeaten for the first time ever. I had my injury problems though, and sometimes I was unavailable for the games; there were also times when I was unhappy with the tactics. But despite all of the things that were said about me at the time in the newspapers, I was never selfish and always had the Dutch national team at heart. I only wanted the very best for them, which is precisely the reason why I felt the team tactics were wrong.

There was a movement in the dressing room which very much wanted Johan Cruyff to replace Libregts and take us to Italia 90, and there were those who were convinced that we would follow up our 1988 European Championships win with a World Cup victory under Cruyff's experienced direction, in the process becoming the undisputed number one country in the world. Naturally enough this became the subject of a huge debate in Holland. The Dutch Federation knew there was dissatisfaction among the players and a desire for a change of style, but Libregts wasn't prepared to stand down, and as captain of the team, with its welfare and contentedness my main concern, I felt I had to do something about a situation which was rapidly getting out of hand and threatening our progress. As a result, the Federation asked the players to vote on the matter: Do you want Libregts to lead Holland into the World Cup, and if not, who? The officials wanted the players to say first if they wanted Libregts, and if they didn't want him they needed the preferred name as a successor. Some twenty squad members cast a vote and, unsurprisingly, announced their desire for Cruyff to replace Libregts.

But, just as at club level during my playing days in Holland, as captain I was the bearer of bad news and everyone likes to shoot the messenger. Many people said the decision was rigged by me and that the vote in favour of Cruyff was a direct result of my grudge about Libregts' apparently racist comment from 1984, but I never once tried to persuade any of the players that Cruyff was the best option – they came to that conclusion themselves. But I got the blame for a joint decision. I didn't care though, I had broad enough shoulders. Of course I had my personal views on Libregts, but as I've said, I have a good sense of responsibility and I distanced myself from those feelings for the benefit of the national team. The vote against Libregts was not about a personal vendetta, it was democracy in action, but naturally people thought I was working on a different agenda.

In retrospect it was a bad decision by the Dutch Federation to allow the players a vote like that. They knew what the problems were, the source of the players' dissatisfaction, and they should have taken the decision either to replace Libregts with Cruyff or keep faith with Libregts themselves. Instead they kept well clear of it and in the public mind it was all down to player power. I can imagine that even now most people think the whole sorry episode was down to my personal dislike for Libregts, but it's just not true.

You can imagine how I felt when just a few weeks before the 1996 FA Cup Final in England one national newspaper quoted Libregts saying some nasty things about me. I was astounded that at such a time he should have been given a platform to launch an attack on me that was completely unfounded and clearly prejudiced – surely that said more about the man himself than me! But he didn't intimidate me – instead I remembered the wise words of Wim van Hanegem and Johan Cruyff: The more you stand up for your rights, the bigger player you are, the more hostility you will face. I just said to myself during these trying periods, 'Okay, Ruud, when you stick up for yourself you know what will happen.' I haven't changed my attitude: I've always done what I felt had to be done, what was right. Unfortunately human beings are all too predictable in the way they react, but I always feel their words reveal more about the way they are than about the subject of the criticism.

Thijs Libregts naturally felt aggrieved by the Dutch players' views and refused to back down, forcing the Dutch Federation to step in and take the whole matter to court, maintaining that there was 'a bad atmosphere between the coach and the players'. The court in Utrecht came to the conclusion that the FA had a point and that Libregts' position was untenable. But if the removal of Libregts was 'player power', we were shorn of it when it came to the replacement. Rinus Michels, now technical adviser for the Dutch Federation, was given the authority to find someone for the World Cup, but he didn't turn to Johan Cruyff in Holland's hour of need – instead his surprise appointment was Leo Beenhakker. The decision left the players feeling deflated. Not that Leo Beenhakker wasn't the right person, but the players believed Johann Cruyff would have been his choice.

Little wonder, then, that when the Dutch team got on the

plane bound for Italy, there was hardly the best of atmospheres on board. And the spirits of the players didn't improve when we arrived at our training pitch in Palermo on the island of Sicily. We had a miserable tournament – awful, considering we were European champions – and were eliminated in the second round by Germany, a match that will be remembered only for an incident between Rudi Voller and Frank Rijkaard. Leo Beenhakker was only assigned for this tournament and after that Michels took on Dick Advocaat as his assistant with the intention of grooming him to take over as the national coach after the European Championships in Sweden in 1992.

Although I was still captain of the side it was a bitter disappointment for me that I didn't play a major role in the qualifying stages for that tournament. In May 1991 I had a recurrence of my knee injuries and Dr Marc Maertens, the Belgian specialist, took out a piece of cartilage and I missed the end of the season. But I was more than happy to leave the ins and outs of my knee problems in the capable hands of Maertens. What I liked, and still like, about him is the way he handles these injuries. He is not one of those doctors who takes the easy option and rushes you into the operating theatre, instead he wants to give the body more time to heal itself and see if he can't help in other ways. If he can't, then of course he'll revert to surgery, but because of his approach he imbues you with confidence and constantly tells you that everything will be fine. Nevertheless, I had to work very hard to make a comeback, but our campaign in Sweden ended very disappointingly. Holland were knocked out in the semi-finals in a penalty shoot-out by the eventual winners of the tournament, Denmark. Michels resigned as a result and, as had been planned, Advocaat assumed the coaching duties.

We were drawn in the same group as England in the qualifying stages for the 1994 World Cup in the United

States. I'd never lost a game against England, and I was very eager to play at Wembley. In fifteen years as a professional footballer I had not played there yet, but the match didn't turn out as I had hoped – far from it. England took the lead with a magnificent free kick from John Barnes, and David Platt scored a second. Dennis Bergkamp brought us back into the game, but Advocaat was far from happy with our performance. He substituted me after an hour's play. I wasn't happy with his decision, and I felt I couldn't go and sit on the bench as if I'd accepted it, so instead I made my way down the Wembley tunnel towards the dressing room. At least the English fans applauded me, which was nice.

The substitution was the culmination of another upsetting time for me with the national team and I genuinely felt as though I'd had enough. After the game I handed in my resignation, and Advocaat accepted it. I didn't play in any of the remaining qualifying games. Of course it's very sad when your international career comes to an end, especially under such circumstances, and deep down you really don't want to do it. But I had to remain true to myself and to my feelings. I'd sat down after that Wembley defeat and thought long and hard about my future with Holland, and decided it was time to say 'Thank you very much' and get on with the rest of my life.

But not long before the World Cup Finals themselves Advocaat felt he couldn't do without me, and I was sure it had a lot to do with the Dutch media campaign mounted to bring me back into the fold. At the time I was playing extremely well at Sampdoria. Advocaat came over to Italy, and after a long chat with him I decided I would join the Dutch squad at their training camp in Noordwijk. I had agreed to return under certain conditions, and I made a pact with the coach that they would be kept between myself and him for the benefit of the team – and that is still the case.

Holland had just the one friendly game remaining before leaving for America, and that was against Scotland in Utrecht. I felt very comfortable playing in the centre of the attack, even though I came off at half-time so the coach could have a last look at other players. But I still was not happy with the tactics of the team and said so in a television interview just after the game. Many people were surprised by what I had to say, considering how well Holland had played on the night, but I had my reasons. The Dutch like to play up front with two wingers, and that kind of strategy needs a lot of hard work and running – fine for Europe, but not in the summertime heat of the USA. Five days later, and only three weeks before the start of the World Cup, a press conference was called; more than a hundred people from the media of more than ten countries gathered at the Hotel Huis ter Duin on the Dutch coast. Ger Stolk, the press officer for the 1994 Dutch World Cup squad, and I sat down and Dick Advocaat announced that I would not be travelling to the United States with Holland and that I was leaving the hotel that morning. The media were shocked by this, but I was in a daze myself – it had been such a momentous decision to take.

Despite all the questions that were thrown at me I refused to give the journalists the answers they wanted. I was thinking all the while about the Dutch team and their preparations for the World Cup, and I didn't want to be the cause of even more disruption, over and above the announcement of my resignation. The decision to quit was mine alone, and I talked with Advocaat the night before and he asked to me to think on it overnight. The next day I hadn't changed my mind, and Advocaat and I decided to call the press conference so that everything would be out in the open. I never played for Holland again.

I disagreed totally with the whole philosophy of how the team was going to play that summer, and it was not within my power to change anything. It felt like having a beautiful car, one that you had coveted for so long, and then finding that you didn't have the key to drive it. I so much wanted to play in the USA but I did not possess that key to unlock the problems within the Dutch camp, and I feared for our chances without it. As I've said, I had very strong views about the way we had to play to combat the extreme heat that teams encountered out there. I was convinced we had the players capable of winning the World Cup, but it was a question of how we utilised them, how we played – we had to play with our brains, not our hearts. The means to do it successfully were within our grasp, and it was a crying shame that they were not realised. Playing very typical Dutch tactics, Holland were not very good at the beginning of the tournament and were lucky to go through to the knock-out stages. By the time they switched to a more realistic 4–4–2 it was too late – they should have done it beforehand and got used to it.

When Brazil played in the 1994 World Championships, the Brazilian press and the people were not happy about the way they played. They thought it wasn't 'Brazilian' enough, there was no flair, it was based too much on defensive tactics – even Pele expressed his opinions thus. As a result enormous pressure was placed on the squad and their coach, Mario Zagalo, to conform to what was widely acknowledged as the traditional Brazilian attacking style. But Zagalo had thought deeply about the difficulties posed by the climate, and the humidity in particular, and had formulated a set of team tactics which he thought would give his team the best chance of success – and hats off to the man. Brazil disposed of Holland on their way to winning their fourth World Cup.

Perhaps Zagalo remembered Brazil's experiences in the 1982 World Championships in Spain, when Brazil met Italy. Several Brazilian players – Falcao, Junior and others – had inside knowledge of the Italians as they were playing in Serie A at the time. Against Italy you don't attack indiscriminately because in those days they employed the *catenaccio* defence pattern – everybody linking together around their own penalty box, waiting for the chance to pounce on a counter-attack. Although they knew this, the majority of the Brazilian team insisted on playing the classic Brazilian all-out attacking game, and the Italians beat them. Moreover, they went on to play some very attractive and very accomplished football themselves, illustrating that they knew precisely when to change tactics for the good of the team. That year Italy won the World Cup.

There was the prospect of little tactical flexibility in the Dutch squad for 1994. One of the problems was that we had a team full of world-class players, all of them big personalities, all of them with their own views. You know the Dutch attitude – we always know better than anyone else! Within the camp everyone had an opinion he wanted to air, and the most overriding view was that the team needed a potent leader, someone with an immense reputation we could all look up to, someone with the necessary clout, skill and experience to instil the discipline Holland so desperately needed, someone who could organise the sort of regime we all wanted – and everyone knew that was Johan Cruyff. The Dutch were at their best with 'The General', Rinus Michels, in charge, and we needed another dominant personality at the helm.

It has always been said about the Dutch that they enjoy a good internal row, that there is nothing like an argument to motivate them. That may be because Dutch players think about the game deeply and have very strong feelings about it as a result. What happened just before the 1994 World Cup was mirrored in many ways by what happened to the Dutch team prior to the 1996 European Championships in England, when the world had another insight into what can happen in the training camp of a national team. Suddenly, all the behind-the-scenes dissent exploded to the surface, out in the open for everyone to see. Edgar Davids was sent home as a result.

Perhaps all this time there has been only one solution to all these problems, although I might only be expressing a personal view: appoint Johan Cruyff as the Dutch national coach. If everyone always clamours for Cruyff when there's a vacancy, then whoever comes in as a replacement instead of him is always, *always*, going to be second choice in the nation's psyche. That cannot be fair to the man who comes in to do a job in his own way. With Cruyff there would be no dissent; if any remained he would sort it out. If this was no longer an issue then the Dutch team stands a very good chance of winning the World Cup.

7
THE COLOUR
OF SKIN

There have been suggestions that the problems in the Dutch camp before the 1994 World Cup and the 1996 European Championships have had something to do with racism, but this was just an easy excuse to deflect public attention away from the real problems. Not that racism hasn't been a problem in football, though, or in the world at large. Violence and racism quite often happen unexpectedly, and when they do the incident can make a big impression on your life, and that happened to me for the first time when I was about fourteen.

There were gangs of youths in every neighbourhood in the capital city at that time, and they roamed the streets menacingly. I had very little to do with them, but one day I was with a black friend of mine and we were strolling through the streets as kids of that age do, with no malicious intent. On occasion when I had been walking like this before

I used to hear the odd nasty comment, a member of a gang shouting out, 'You black bastard, you can't walk around here'; that kind of thing. But this time I was shocked and surprised to see that the guy with me, as I said a friend of mine and a member of my school, was carrying a bicycle pump that had been sharpened at the end so that it resembled an ice-pick. It was a horrible-looking weapon, and I kept on asking myself, 'Why does he have it?' As usual some guy started shouting racist remarks at us, and when my friend heard these taunts he pulled out the sharpened pump and confronted them. It was more the terror of that moment than anything that stays with me – there was no fight or any actual contact at all. I remember shouting at him, 'You can't do this sort of shit'; all I wanted to do was separate them and get the hell out of there. I just wanted it to be over. There was quite a loud stir and eventually the police arrived to break it up, and they took us into custody.

We were taken to police headquarters and searched. I was just a school kid with a head full of football at the time, and I was carrying nothing incriminating, but the thing which really hurt me was the way I was treated by the police. I distinctly recall one of them asking me if I had any books, and then saying, 'I suppose the nigger *can* read?' I was shocked. Horrified. I just thought to myself, You can't talk to me like that, and I told him so. All he said in reply was, 'Well, the nigger has a big mouth.' It was bad enough being detained in the police station – I'd never been to one before – but I was trembling after what he said to me. They kept us there for a short time before letting us go. When I got home it was very difficult for me to explain to my mother what had happened. My mother is white, but I am her son and she went berserk. She was livid that I should be treated in such a disgusting way, and immediately stormed off to the police headquarters. She went absolutely mad when she got there and told the police officer exactly what she thought of him, but she never told me exactly what she said.

That was my first direct experience of racism, and I can tell you, it wasn't an easy thing to cope with. It was a totally bemusing experience, and I think I grew up a bit quicker as a result of it. It was certainly a turning point for me, because I started to realise what the real world was all about. For so long I had experienced only the good things in life, but now I knew there were bad things as well. I remember few details about the incident itself, but I do recall being paralysed with fear when I saw that bicycle pump being brandished, and the knives that came out in response. I'd been cocooned in a completely different, loving world, and I had never been in trouble. Of course, like all boys of that age I had had bad times at school, cracked one joke too many in class and been reprimanded for bad behaviour, but this was something on a completely different plane. Suddenly I realised why these guys were in gangs and why people like that carried knives and baseball bats.

Although it's an aspect of my life that I will never forget, it is also something I try to put to the back of my mind, although without as much success as I'd like. In the Jordaan race and colour were not issues, and it was some time after I began my career in football that I experienced my first racist incident in sport.

The fourteenth of September 1983, to be precise. That was the date of my first European game, a UEFA Cup second-round tie with Feyenoord against St Mirren in Scotland. It was the first time I'd ever been to Scotland and I was looking forward to it very much, but from the moment I first walked onto the pitch it was just so strange – the fans were shouting all sorts of names at me. When I was warming up they were hurling abuse at me too. It came as such a shock to me. I wasn't all that far from home, but it was as if I had been transported to a different world. I was the only black player in the Feyenoord team, so clearly I stood out as a target; I was perhaps one of the first black players ever to play for a European team on Scottish turf. It certainly affected me, but I managed to channel it into positive rather than negative energy. I had a good match that night and scored the goal in a 1–0 win, a very good goal as I recall, and that I thought was a fitting response to the racists in the crowd. I should say that the taunting was the work of a minority, as always – after the match the coach and chairman of St Mirren were very embarrassed and apologetic.

Because I had come through that experience so well, with my dignity intact (we beat them in the return leg too, 2–0), from that moment on whenever it happened to me again I would see things from a different point of view: I didn't feel insulted, I just felt sorry for those who felt the need to say such things. Taunting verged on the intolerable in those days, and sometimes fans would call you a 'black c—t', or tell you to 'get back on the banana boat'. I've never felt intimidated by that sort of language, it was just a group of people making fools of themselves. It's a sign of ignorance and fear, and perhaps also indicative of the fact that they are afraid of me as a footballer in some way, afraid of what I might do to their team. They don't have to be afraid, of course, and I don't believe such behaviour is as prevalent in football today as it was in those days, and when it happens it is always accompanied by a great deal of public and official outrage. Ajax were recently in Hungary to play Ferencvaros in a Champions League group match, and all the black players were booed and jeered at whenever they touched the ball; as a result Ferencvaros were reported to FIFA for bad behaviour.

When I signed for Chelsea and came to England I was told how prevalent racism used to be in football in this country, and that Chelsea was among the clubs to have suffered badly from it, but it was so difficult to imagine when I was at the club. I was told that Stamford Bridge was a renowned breeding ground for the National Front and that racism was a problem, and that although such ignorance didn't really exist anymore you can never be complacent about combating it as an issue because it can always be just around the next corner. Seeing kids come along to matches at Stamford Bridge during my time there to watch football in a good environment and a healthy, family atmosphere always pleased me. The kids are football's future, and it is important that adults set them the right standards in terms of behaviour, so that they can learn inside a stadium about good, wholesome sporting principles.

Ignorance can come in many forms, of course: people can feel threatened in terms of their jobs, livelihoods or social lives, and feel that they need someone to blame – it's that kind of mentality. The same sort of thing happened in Holland in the 1970s. The Dutch people felt a whole number of jobs such as cleaning the streets were beneath them, so the country imported large numbers of immigrants from Turkey and Morocco to undertake the menial tasks. Identical problems have occurred at some time in virtually every country in the world. Fifteen years on, with unemployment rising, people began to say, 'They've taken the jobs we should be doing.'

Since those experiences on the streets of Amsterdam and at St Mirren and elsewhere, I have always been willing to stand up for the rights of any oppressed minority. I was approached one day by Irika Terpstra, the Dutch Minister for Sport, and she outlined to me a new Dutch government initiative to create a position which would be called the Ambassador for Intolerance in Sport, and would I be interested in taking up the post and lending my name to the campaign? Of course, I said yes, and they can use my name for this purpose and on occasion I will attend conferences and other official functions in support of the initiative, but they appreciate I can't be with them all the time because I have to get on with my life – but I always help as much as I can because it's an issue that's very close to my heart.

Maybe I never had any role models in football, or even in sport generally, but I did have one hero in my life – Nelson Mandela. When I lived in Holland I used to contribute to a programme on a station called Radio Vara which supported the work in South Africa of the African National Congress (ANC), particularly its Free Nelson Mandela campaign. I did guest spots on the radio show with a whole lot of other celebrities who were committed to the cause.

On one such occasion I met a man, Sam Ramsey, who was a member of a group connected with the ANC. During our conversation Sam said something to me that I found quite curious at the time, but which made me rethink the reasons why I was doing what I was doing and the way in which I was going about it. He said, 'Ruudi, I don't want you to go on every TV programme that asks you, or on the radio all the time. People know where you stand on this issue, now that you have made your statement of intent. The best thing you can do for us is play good football.' After considering these words I realised I knew exactly what he meant: I could do more on behalf of the anti-apartheid movement and for Nelson Mandela by being a high-profile, adulated sports star than I could by just spouting words into a microphone.

What I couldn't really understand was why Nelson Mandela had been in prison for so long – around the same number of years as I had been alive. I felt the obvious injustice of it, and when I won the World and European Footballer of the Year awards in 1987 I dedicated those honours to his name. Considering I'd always been associated publicly with the campaign against apartheid in South Africa, I never imagined the impact such a gesture would have around the world. I was genuinely surprised by all the supportive words. Everyone seemed to go crazy about it and I spent all day on radio and TV talking about why I'd done it. Holland was one of the first countries to come out and fight against the racialist regime in South Africa. So it was something normal to make such a dedication, but I can understand why to the rest of the world it must have seemed an unusual, even brave, thing to do, and why there was such intense interest in it at the time. However, by that time my experiences in club and international football had more than adequately equipped me to absorb all the media pressure and take it in my stride, but it had a profound effect on me in many ways, and from that day on I was resolved to meet Nelson Mandela face to face.

The first time that happened was when we were brought together for a TV programme in Holland not long after he had been released from prison in 1990. We met just prior to the show's transmission in the TV studios and I asked him if I could meet him privately a little later on. In fact, we met privately for around half an hour. It was something I'd always wanted to do, especially so in the previous couple of years, and I wasn't disappointed when it happened. I asked him many personal questions – I was just so curious about his life – and he was very gracious and understanding with his answers.

He also paid me a great compliment. When I toured South Africa with the Dutch national team in the summer of 1997 to play a match in his honour, Mandela bestowed upon me the highest accolade in South Africa by making me a Commander of the Order of Good Hope in the large directors' lounge in the stadium where South Africa v. Holland was taking place. When I went on stage to be presented with this prize, I've never felt so proud in all my life. Also on stage that day was Miss South Africa, and the real compliment

Mandela paid me was when he turned to her and, pointing at people like me, said, 'These are the real warriors who have worked so hard and relentlessly against apartheid, and they are the ones who have succeeded. Now that it's gone there are so many people who want to join the fight, when it's too late.' And he looked at me when he added, 'These guys dedicated themselves to the real struggle.' Well, no one could have paid me greater praise, and that includes my European and World Footballer of the Year awards.

Fortunately, before Mandela made his little speech I had had a chance to talk to him, albeit very briefly, on the stage. When Miss South Africa was introduced to him he kissed her on both cheeks, and I said, 'Hey! It's good to be a president!' We all laughed at that. But I was certainly speechless after that – he was one of my heroes, a man I'd looked up to and respected, and he was saying such warm and generous things about me. I was so proud of what he said to me, so touched inside, and at the same time it was a very strange feeling. I was like a child again – I could have easily put my thumb in my mouth. I had gone weak at the knees. You know me, I'm never lost for words, but I struggled to find a single word to utter. And in addition to all that I went to Mandela's former house in Soweto where a number of secret meetings with the ANC had taken place before his arrest. I was hugely privileged indeed.

I admired Nelson Mandela for many reasons, but not necessarily just because I'm black. I've met a whole lot of white people I've admired too. And I would have the same feelings towards Mandela whatever our colour – because it's just as much about injustice, which can take many different forms, as it is about race. Nelson Mandela is an easy man to admire because he just has lots of natural charisma, and few people in this world have such qualities. Princess Diana was one, and she is a person I admired greatly too. People who possess those qualities are always greatly loved.

There was a guy who accompanied me in South Africa when I travelled there with the national team, and he told me many stories about Mandela, but there was one in particular I shall always cherish. He told me how one day during a debate in the South African parliament Mandela had shown his enormous intelligence when out of the blue he made a marvellous observation. He suggested there were three types of people in the world. There's the guy that works hard, goes home, loves his wife and children, he's a great family man but nobody knows him. There's a second type who also excels at his job and works well, but when people hear his name they feel love and affection for him. When they see him everybody adores him. Thirdly, there's the type of guy that whenever you hear his name it sends a shiver down your spine because you are so afraid of him. Sometimes you hate him. Mandela then told all these government officials: 'Now it's up to you, in the years you still have ahead of you, to make up your own minds which of these people you want to be for the rest of your life, and how all of those close to you and everybody else will remember you when you die.'

That really got to me, I thought it was such a very good statement to have made – and in front of all those people in a government building! What a speech that was, so commanding and so profound. And which one of these three would I like to be? Well, I suppose we all want to be loved, but you have to do something to deserve that love. The Dutch have a saying: 'If you do right you receive good.'

8

CHELSEA HERE
I COME

My decision to leave Italy for Chelsea was made from the heart and the head, and the reason for that was that my life in Italy at this time was in a mess, full of personal, private problems. I played my last season in Italian football, 1994/5, with Sampdoria, and although I had plenty of a footballing nature to occupy my mind – the club won the Italian Cup that season – few people, only those very close to me, knew the details and extent of the emotional ructions going on.

I was very low at the time for a number of reasons. Some of it had to do with my return to Milan for a short while in the middle of a very bizarre 1993/4 season. I went back because the club approached me to say that they'd made a mistake by selling me too early and would I return, and Milan was still dear to my heart. What I achieved at Milan was very similar, I felt in retrospect, to what I achieved at

Chelsea – the sense that you are building something of your own, almost, and the obvious pride you have in that is very addictive. That's how I saw it, so when Milan offered to have me back, I didn't really hesitate. I was also delighted by the club's reaction, because it meant my mission had been accomplished: I had proved to them conclusively that my knees were not made of glass and that I still had a lot to give to a big club. When I went back to Milan I was in very good shape, but Milan at that time was not playing so well. In one game against Lazio with just four minutes to go they equalised to make the score 1–1. Then just one minute before the end I scored a winner. The newspapers were all shouting that Gullit was the only one who could save Milan. The previous year Milan had won the Italian Championship and the Champions' League and now suddenly it was Gullit is the only one who can save us? Well, it was at that moment that the problems began. I had a meeting with the vice-president of Milan, Mr Galliani, at which I spelled out the problems I had with the footballing side of things at the club, and I told him that if Milan felt they could not resolve these problems then I would appreciate being put on a free transfer again. I really did want to stay, but the whole episode didn't work out, and I must confess that when I returned to Sampdoria three months later I was a nervous wreck. For the first two weeks I couldn't play football. Fortunately for me there were some very kind people at Sampdoria, the family club, and they knew I was in torment. I entrusted my innermost feelings to them and uncannily they knew exactly what my situation was and how I had to deal with it.

When I came to the end of the season, a decision had to be made, and it was a very, very difficult one for me – primarily because I was a public figure and I was painfully aware that whatever I did would affect those closest to me. You know, there are so many pressures in life to conform to some ideal: so many women want to look like models, for instance, and so many men want to be famous footballers or cash-rich businessmen. People enjoy being in the spotlight – so long as it's temporary – and it's this quest for 'glamour' that has created an unquenchable thirst for gossip. Ordinary people can feel that they share the same sort of problems as the rich and famous, for instance, and feel better for it. They can say to themselves, 'That guy might have everything he's ever craved, but he still has his problems, whatever they might be.' There's always going to be a desire to delve into the private lives of the rich and famous, because people will always feel that need to close the gap between 'them and us' a bit. So whenever a high-profile person has to make a decision in his or her life, you have to consider all the possible repercussions before you take that step, otherwise life could get even worse.

My first thoughts were for my children. I had two kids from my first marriage – Felicity and Charmayne – and now my second marriage was breaking up and I had to think of my two other children, Quincy and Cheyenne, too. Those closest to me knew what was going on at the time and the agony I was going through trying to make the right choices in life, and they supported and sympathised with me. But there came a time when I had to look in the mirror and say, 'Okay, Ruud, you've done everything you can, now act.' It wasn't the place – I hadn't fallen out of love with Italy – it was the circumstances. I had an Italian wife and I'd gone through a bad time with the Milan club, and the combination of the two had driven me virtually crazy. I just *had* to do something about it.

I'm not a religious man, but I was so depressed at one stage that I went to the St Francis Church in Milan where the monks allow everybody in regardless of religious persuasion or culture. There I met Father Robert and I spoke to him at

121

great length. I asked him all kinds of questions because I was at the end of my tether. He could not really give me any straight answers, of course, but he told me that life's problems can be solved through the words of the Bible. He touched me somehow, and our discussion opened up my mind to a number of things. He told me to try to be a bigger man and to be more appreciative of the good things in life. Often I would go to the church alone when I knew the place would be empty, just so that I could sit down and think in peace and quiet. It did help me. Sometimes I sat there for two hours, asking myself the same questions over and over again and racking my brain for solutions: Why did some people seem to want to do nasty things to me? How was it possible that people I once trusted and loved could turn against me? I went down every possible avenue and convinced myself that I had done all in my power to avoid these things. Of course I accepted my limitations – we all have to. I am a person who gives everything. I may not always make the right decisions, but at least I am aware that I make mistakes and I always give people who have made their own mistakes the time and space in which to rectify them.

It's weird, you know. People always think I'm Mr Cool, more laid back and relaxed than anyone else. It's certainly a reputation I have on the football field, but it's simply not true. I feel the stress and tension of a big game just as much as the next person, and it's the same in life. I just like to express myself in a different way: some people feel the need to scream and shout, I prefer to stay as calm as I can and think about things. But Ruud Gullit is the same as everybody; there are some things you just can't cope with without help.

By mid-1995 I was feeling so lonely: I didn't have a proper routine of my own yet, but at the same time it felt as though everyone lived with me. Being such a high-profile person, it was impossible to keep the sorry developments in my personal and professional lives out of the newspapers, and I hated the constant gossip and speculation in the media and having to listen to or read people's opinions on private matters wherever I went. I had a deep conviction that the only way to shake myself out of the despair in which I wallowed was to do something completely different with my life – I had to become Ruud Gullit again; I had to find myself again. So it was precisely the right moment when Glenn Hoddle rang me in May 1995 to ask me to come and join Chelsea. I was impressed by his ideas and was attracted by the thought of moving to London. I've always sought new challenges, and there had never been a time in my life when I'd needed one more; moreover, he wanted me to fit in to the Chelsea side as a sweeper, a role I was happy to play. I didn't tell Glenn anything about my personal problems at the time because I knew I was ready to throw myself into a new adventure.

I still remember his first telephone call to me a few months before – Sampdoria were playing Cagliari in Sardinia at the time. He said, 'Hi, I'm Glenn Hoddle from Chelsea,' to which I replied, 'What!?' He explained that he was the Chelsea manager and that he wanted to sign me and would like to have talks with me about a move to London. 'Okay,' I said, 'come over to Milan and see me whenever you like. Just call me first and we'll arrange a meeting.' I got on with my life, or what was left of it, afterwards and heard nothing more. Then I thought about it. Chelsea! Of course I'd heard of the club, but I didn't have much idea about the place or the team. The fact that I didn't hear anything for a while made me think that the opportunity had disappeared.

Then one day I had to go to the Milan offices on business. I was sitting there in one of the rooms inside the club, and this guy was sitting there as well. I couldn't recall his name, but I recognised him as a players' representative because I'd seen him around the club before and knew he acted as an agent. He began to talk to me, and started to discuss a number of clubs that might be interested in me. First he mentioned Paris St Germain and that they'd pay a lot of money to secure my services. What is this? I thought to myself. It seemed strange that he should be talking to me about transfers and moves to different countries – I'd never really met him and I still don't know his name. I thought he was just chatting, but then he said to me, 'Have you got a move organised?' I told him I hadn't, and he replied, 'Well, do you know that Glenn Hoddle is here?'

'No, I didn't.'

'Yeah, he's in my office, would you like to come and talk to him?'

Well, you can imagine how astonished I was, and a bit piqued, so I said, 'I'm sorry, but I have no time at the moment – in fact I've got to go. I had no appointment with Glenn Hoddle.'

'No, no, no, wait a minute,' he spluttered.

He was very insistent that I should stay, so I thought I'd humour him and hang around a bit. I waited for about ten minutes, and then Glenn Hoddle and Colin Hutchinson, Chelsea's managing director, walked into the room. I said hello but explained that they were lucky to have found me there. They said that the guy I'd been speaking to had said he was my manager and had arranged for this meeting to take place. Again, I was astonished – I couldn't believe what was going on. I told them in no uncertain terms that this guy was not my manager and that I knew nothing about an appointment. Now it was their turn to be astonished. My suggestion was that we arranged another meeting ourselves, which we did. Players' agents can behave incredibly at times. They can set up all sorts of meetings and say they are acting for all kinds of players, just to get deals going and claim a piece of the pie. I was linked with all sorts of clubs – Galatasaray, Bayern Munich, Monaco, Feyenoord, even the Japanese club Yokohama Flugels. At least, that's what I read in the papers.

Glenn, Colin and I met at a nice hotel in Milan, a much more comfortable environment in which to chat about business and away from everyone inside the football club. We got on well and for the first time in a long while I felt that my life was going to change for the better. I was ready to sign for Chelsea.

However, I had to make a trip to Hong Kong and China with Sampdoria before then as an end-of-season tour. With my future virtually settled in my mind it was a really lovely trip. I had a wonderful time, and after the tour ended I moved on to Japan for some promotional work. That gave me the opportunity to invite out my best friends: Gengiro Miyakou, who's half-Japanese and half-Italian, and Ewald van der Bogt. We spent a week in Tokyo and the three of us had a great time. My friends knew what a hard time I'd been through and they'd always stayed close to me, and they were pleased about my news of Chelsea. During that week I flourished again as a person; everything was new out there and I had it all to look forward to. In fact, I couldn't wait to get back to Italy, pack up my stuff and get off to England.

It turned out to be a difficult departure. My biggest regret was leaving the kids – my ex-wife was awarded custody of them by the court – but I also felt sorry saying goodbye to the people at Sampdoria, who had been so good to me. Also, despite all the ups and downs, I had been in Italian football for eight years, and it was a bit of a wrench just to close a large chapter of my life. But I was desperately looking forward to a fresh life in London, so you can imagine my excitement when I boarded the flight to Gatwick. When I arrived at the airport I was picked up by Terry Byrne, a representative of the club and whisked off to Stamford Bridge. It was a bright Thursday, 22 June 1995, when I started my new life and career.

You wouldn't believe how I felt when I first saw the ground. At the time it was undergoing major refurbishment work, and when I walked in it was only in the embryonic stages of a massive redevelopment plan. But this was my first acquaintance with the scheme, and I hadn't been led to expect only half a club when I arrived. When I first laid eyes on the stadium there were builders crawling all over it, and I remember thinking: What am I doing? Inside the ground there was rubble all over the place, and to get round you had to use interconnecting planks of wood. For the last eight years I had been used to the opulence of the top Italian clubs, but I hardly recognised Stamford Bridge as a Premier League stadium at all – it was a complete mess, a total wreckage, an absolute disgrace.

It didn't get any better when I walked into Drakes restaurant in the new stand for my first press conference in England, and sat next to my new manager, Glenn Hoddle. The first question I was asked was about Wimbledon. 'Yeah,' I replied, 'they play very good tennis there.' Everyone laughed and thought I was making some dry comic statement, but I wasn't joking at all. Of course I knew of the existence of a football club at Wimbledon, but I didn't know what the journalist was hinting at because I knew nothing about how they played the game there. So when I was asked about Wimbledon I just assumed they meant the famous tennis championships – it was the first thing that came into my mind. It was Glenn who leant over and whispered that they were making an allusion to the football club. So I just said, 'I'm looking forward to playing there. It's one of the most important stadiums in the world.' Oh dear. Then I added, 'Perhaps I should talk about tennis as well?'

After the press conference the club sent me to the lovely Conrad Hotel in Chelsea harbour. I stayed there for a day, went back home for a bit, and then went on holiday to Portugal. I played golf every day and relaxed, all by myself. I had a big bungalow and I spent a fortnight there. I spent a lot of my time reading – my favourite authors are thriller writers like Frederick Forsyth and Stephen King – and I trained every day, running relentlessly on the beach, determined to prepare myself physically before my return to Chelsea. I'd never played in English football, of course, but I'd heard all about its reputation as a physically demanding league. There was a lovely restaurant out on the beach with a Brazilian owner, and I enjoyed long lunches there basking in some fantastic weather. They always seemed to be playing really relaxing, smooth music, and emotionally it was easy for me to unwind. I'll never forget the endless Sade tapes, which are now among my favourite music. Music has always been part of my life and certain records remind me of particular times. When I was at Sampdoria, for instance, one record always stood out for me – Karen White's 'I'd Rather Be Alone'. It meant so much to me at the time that I played it every day. If you listen to the words of that record you'll understand why.

Finally I returned utterly refreshed to Chelsea for the start of the new 1995/6 season. Every time you go to a new club it is always strange at first. I'm sure the players looked at me and thought 'flashy git'; they probably thought I had my nose in the air and that I looked down it at them – and it is quite a big nose – and there was some tension in the air to begin with, but it only took a couple of days' socialising to get rid of it. On the practical side, I've always realised the implications of my status in the game and the expectations that follow me around are always going to be very high, which is why I prepared myself so thoroughly on holiday. I was determined that no one would think I was just along for the ride.

At first I lived in a hotel in Slough with Sparky – Mark Hughes. At my first press conference when I signed for Chelsea it was announced that Hughes would also be joining the club, from Manchester United. I was glad of the company in that hotel because there was nothing to do. Hotel life was boring and I spent most of my time out and about looking at houses in London. Fortunately, after a very short time I had my eyes firmly trained on one.

I hadn't been in Slough very long when, driving back to the hotel one day from the training ground at Harlington, I decided on the spur of the moment to go and see what London was really like, so I followed the M4 down into the heart of the capital, and when I saw signs for the city I made directly for Piccadilly. It wasn't an easy trip because everyone seemed to drive on the wrong side of the street, and I had a few bumps taking the curves and getting used to the roads, but it was a lovely summer's evening. I wound down the windows, and when I first caught sight of Piccadilly Circus I said to myself, 'This is it.' I just had that feeling: 'Yeah, this is the right place for me. I made the right decision.' I seem to have this sixth sense sometimes, and when I had these good vibes about the city my mind was made up once and for all, and I knew I was going to enjoy my time at Chelsea. I moved into my new house not long after that and, although I was lonely at times, all my former enthusiasm for the game returned.

It wasn't long before I was making new friends at Chelsea. Right from the beginning captain Dennis Wise, coach Gwyn Williams and I played a lot of golf together. At first it was a bit difficult to understand Dennis, and it took a while to catch on to his Cockney way of speaking, but eventually I understood him perfectly. It used to give me so much pleasure to beat Gwyn at golf. He told me that he was a regular player, and a good one too, and that I must have

Top: One of the great moments of my career, Captain of the Netherlands when we won the 1988 European Championships in Germany

Above: Watching fellow Dutch Internationals in a friendly match in preparation for the 1990 World Cup Finals in Italy

Left: Discussing tactics with National coach, Leo Beenhakker

I line up along with Uefa bosses at the Adidas presentation awards in Paris, 1990. PSV Eindhoven won the award for best team

Proudly displaying my award together with Marco van Basten, winner of the Golden Boot, at the same awards. Also in picture are Marco's wife and Johann Cruyff

The first time I met Nelson Mandela was in a television studio when I dedicated my award for World Footballer of the Year to him

Glenn Hoddle was the reason I decided to move to Chelsea from Sampdoria

Left: In the days when I *really* did have pace to burn. My form at PSV Eindhoven attracted a world record £5.5 million bid from AC Milan

Above: It was a privilege to meet Pele when he visited Stamford Bridge. This photo was taken at the party afterwards

Left: Nobody can take away from me the sheer pleasure and pride of being the first foreign coach to win a trophy in English football

Right: I don't normally enjoy wearing ties, but this was a black tie event for the charity *Sparks*. And doesn't Estelle look the business in this Versace dress?

Rudi Gullit and Estelle Cruyff
are delighted to announce
the birth of their daughter

Joëlle Gullit

on Tuesday 18th November 1997
weighing 7 pounds

Joelle means 'yes God' in Dutch, and both Estelle and I were proud to announce the arrival of our lovely baby daughter. Here we are together in our London home been the first black man to have played so well against him. In fact, I spanked Gwyn's backside. *Spanked* it. It was all in such good fun, and, thank God, I was really enjoying life again.

I had been through a very rough time living on my own and sometimes I overreacted even when people tried to be nice to me. I couldn't trust anyone, especially after what had happened in Italy in my job and my private life. The people at Chelsea knew I was alone and that I was searching for something in London, the sort of freedom I used to enjoy in Amsterdam, where I could walk down the streets and no one bothered me. My whole perspective on life was changed by London, where people seemed to understand my difficulties and gave me my space.

I was on my own for my first Christmas in London, but the people at the club knew I would end up sitting by myself in my new house, and they weren't going to let that happen. Terry Byrne, the club physio, said to me, 'No, no, you're not going to be on your own, you've got to come with me.' So we all had Christmas together at his mother-in-law's. We had a good time, and I am very grateful to these people for inviting me to their home. Loneliness threatened again on New Year's Eve, but my friend Ewald invited me over to Amsterdam for the celebrations, and I accepted. The only problem was, I was due for training with the other guys on New Year's Day. I didn't manage any sleep that night, and the next day I caught a nine a.m. flight, arriving at Heathrow at nine a.m., pathetically grateful for that hour's time difference. I made my way directly to Harlington, which is about ten minutes' drive away from Heathrow. Training was due to start at 10.45, so I spent just over an hour sleeping on the medical bench. Terry found me there just before training and woke me up.

I hadn't had a drink the night before, nor did I smoke – I

don't smoke anyway – but I was absolutely exhausted. I couldn't train; there was no way I could train, I thought. But, as they say in Holland, 'Big guy at night, big guy in the morning.' I got myself off the medical bench, poured some coffee inside me, and went off to train. In any case, I knew the manager would hammer me if I didn't. A big-name player has to set an example for the others – it didn't matter how dreadful I felt, how tired, or how much I wanted just to go home to bed. No one would have known how I felt that morning because I was determined to be the best that day. But after training I went home and slept from two o'clock that afternoon until the next morning.

I'm very disciplined and believe I am very professional in my attitude towards football, and that New Year was a rare lapse; normally I am very strict with myself – a legacy of my upbringing and Italian training regimes. I remember playing in the following match against Queens Park Rangers – I fell awkwardly on my back and injured myself. I had been playing well up to then, and had attempted an ill-advised scissor kick. Some of the players said it happened because I was out all night over the New Year, but that had nothing to do with it. But the mickey-taking was good – it was just the sort of thing to take me out of myself. I was finding Chelsea to be a really happy environment. The move had turned into the perfect solution to all my problems, and it was going to get even better before the end came.

9
MY PRIVATE LIFE

When Chelsea arranged a pre-
season fixture with my old club Feyenoord in the summer of
1995, it proved to be another turning point in my life.

The team arrived on a Thursday evening, 11 August, in
Rotterdam, and I had a very emotional return to the club on
the Saturday. Feyenoord were just opening their newly
refurbished stadium and a crowd of 38,000 turned up.
During the warm-up the club made a special presentation as
this was my first major game as a player at Feyenoord since I
left, and they made me make a speech. It was a very
emotional moment – it was at Feyenoord that I won my first
championship medal and cup, and the club will always be
special to me.

It never ceases to amaze me how everyone in England
thinks we are all so randy in Holland. While we were staying
in that hotel in Rotterdam for the match the players would
come down to their meals, point at me and say, 'Incredibly
filthy bastard.' They were referring to all the pornographic
channels on their hotel television sets, but they're not there

133

for the Dutch, they're there for the tourists. I said to them, 'You don't have to watch it,' but for some strange reason they all seemed to be late for their meals. 'What a filthy country this is,' they'd say, and I'd reply, 'Why is everyone late for lunch?' It was all good banter and we laughed our heads off as we took the mickey out of each other.

After the match I went with Frank Sinclair, Andy Myers and Eddie Newton to the capital for a night out. I wanted to meet all my old Dutch friends, and we did just that, joining up with people like Edgar Davids and Patrick Kluivert. Dennis Wise wanted to go with us, but because he was injured he didn't get permission. I'm sure Glenn knew that we were going, but in any case we were all in a good mood when we set off for Amsterdam, and we had an enjoyable evening out at a trendy bar, a nice place where you can go for a chat and a cappuccino.

It was at this bar on this night that I bumped into Estelle. I'd met her once before because she was Johan Cruyff's niece, and I knew her father Hennie, Johan's brother, but it was no more than a formal introduction. When we met that night in Amsterdam we had a chance for a chat, but there was nothing serious about it, and to be perfectly frank at that stage in my life I didn't want or need another relationship. I was still very bitter about the way things had worked out in Italy with my ex-wife, and to be honest I was still a bit suspicious and mistrustful around women – certainly not hostile, but wary. I was perfectly happy with my four children, but otherwise rather disturbed by events in my last marriage.

When I first met Estelle, as I've said, I didn't really know her very well and although we got on brilliantly there was nothing romantic going on. Then a few months later I met her again at a New Year's Eve party, the one my friend Ewald had dragged me out of London for. We got on great again, but still there was nothing more to it than being good friends and being able to talk easily with each other. We saw each other again on several occasions after this, but it wasn't until we were together for the celebrations for the Queen of Holland's birthday on 31 May 1996 that things began to change between us. That was the first time I really tried my best to explain to Estelle how and why I'd lost my faith in women, and how the wounds would need time to heal. I wanted to be honest with her; I wanted her to grasp the nettle of all that had gone on in my life. Here was this guy who had kids here and kids there, and who as a consequence had to juggle everything around. Basically, I wanted to let her know what she might be letting herself in for, and it wasn't an easy thing to explain, even to someone as attentive and understanding as Estelle. As I spoke of these intensely private matters which had so upset me during my last years in Italy, Estelle said she just couldn't believe it. I can understand why she was sceptical, and later she tried to establish the truth of what I had said to her by speaking to members of my family and my closest friends, all of whom confirmed every word. I wasn't upset by this – as I said, I can understand why she thought it all too outrageous.

Gradually Estelle came to understand my formerly stand-offish ways with her, and why it had taken me nearly a year since our first meeting to ask her out on an official date. In all the intervening time, apart from a kiss and a cuddle, I didn't touch her once. Now we've had a chance to talk about it it's become one big laugh between us because she has told me, in all seriousness, 'I thought you were a poof!' Can you imagine it – Rudi, a poof! But I can understand why she thought it: Estelle is a beautiful young woman and she didn't know anything about how I had suffered emotionally.

So you might think, what changed my attitude? Estelle's qualities changed my attitude. For the first time in my life a woman provided something which gave me a feeling of serenity and tranquillity within. What I mean by that is I don't have to make an effort all the time to please her, so when I am with her I feel no strain at all. We seem to gel together, we enjoy each other's company and it seems to be the right mix.

Let me give you an example from that night on 31 May, the Queen's birthday, about what I mean when I say it's no strain to be with her. I had English friends of mine over and some close friends from Holland such as Frank Rijkaard. Estelle, of course, was there too. I felt responsible that she should have a great time and that I should entertain her. It was a big party. I was standing there having a laugh with friends and thinking, I hope Estelle is doing well. But I needn't have worried because when I looked over in her direction she was having just as good a time talking to people as I was. Come on, you've all done it – husbands and wives, boyfriends and girlfriends – you are always worried if your partner is feeling bored, and constantly wondering, Does he/she want to go home? And if your partner wants to leave, you have to go as well. I looked at Estelle that night, having a good time, and I felt a warm, comfortable feeling inside.

Sometimes in relationships that involve high-profile personalities the other partner can find it difficult to control his or her jealous instincts, especially if you are the centre of attention. But people in my position *have* to talk to other people – if you ignore them you are accused, often publicly, of all kinds of things. If the partner of a celebrity cannot understand or get accustomed to that simple fact, then the relationship is always going to have problems.

Apart from on the golf course, the only time I can be myself and totally unwind is in Estelle's company. Sometimes she can't understand how I can sit at home for an hour at a time, just thinking. I might have the television on and be facing it, but really I'm just staring at it, a hundred thoughts totally unconnected with the programme whizzing through my head. Sometimes you need that peace of mind, the space to meditate. There can be so many things on your mind that when you are in your place of work it always becomes too jumbled, too complicated.

Isn't it funny, though, that women have this knack of being able to talk all the time? They don't really attach much importance to being solitary and contemplative. It was the same with my mother years ago when I was small. I would often spend as much time as I do now on my own, thinking, but my mother would ask me if anything was the matter. Of course there wasn't, but like most women my mother thought that if I wasn't doing something or saying something I must be miserable. If my mother was out of the house, she probably suspected that I'd use the time to get friends round and have a party. But I didn't – I just chilled out in front of the television, thinking. I'm just the same person I've always been; I don't think anything has changed me, not the fame nor the trappings of success that go with it. I don't need to be going out every night, dressing up and playing the part. What they see is what they get. I like to be relaxed, and that's why I enjoy wearing casual clothes, not because I think they particularly suit me (although I'm sure they do!). That's why I don't often wear ties, but it's not true to say that I never wear ties: when I was at Chelsea I wore a club tie to the matches along with all the other players.

I am sure people have their thoughts about football players, and I've no doubt they have their views about me, but all I know is that the people who are closest to me – my friends and my family – know me as I am. Certainly when I get to know new people they seem so surprised that I'm the same person in private as the one up there on the television screen being interviewed after matches, or in the BBC studios sitting next to Des Lynam. I don't talk any differently, I don't pretend to be something I'm not, and I say the things I believe in whether it's to a camera, a microphone, a telephone or a face.

I talk to Estelle about a whole range of things and I'm lucky to have such a good relationship with her at that level. I also have an honest, open relationship with her: we trust each other implicitly, we're committed to each other. For instance, if I say, 'Oh, look at her, she's a beautiful woman,' Estelle wouldn't be in the least bit offended, as I know some women might be. Equally, she can say to me, 'Hey, that's a nice-looking guy,' and I might agree or disagree. It would simply be a point of conversation between us, and wouldn't mean anything other than that. I can't see any other way of leading a normal, healthy life. That's normal to me – you can't be a different person to suit different occasions, you've got to be yourself.

There's something else I ought to mention about Estelle that caught my attention right from the start. It might be an aspect of a relationship that few people would give much importance to, but for me it is indicative of some of the simpler things in life. When you first share a meal with somebody it can tell you a lot about your partner. It struck me instantly about Estelle that she eats everything. You know when someone is putting on some sort of pretence, nibbling at a salad even if they're not hungry or they hate it, just to make an impression of some sort? Not Estelle. There's nothing left when Estelle gets tucked into her food. I love it. I just thought to myself, I've finally found somebody here who just wants to be herself. We share a love of Indonesian food – extremely popular in Holland – and that was the first meal we enjoyed together.

It's just another blissful illustration of how I don't need to be concerned about her. When I'm having a good time I don't continuously have to think about whether she's got a headache, isn't enjoying herself, or wants to go home. As I've already made clear, I don't wish to discuss the ins and outs of my relationships with my ex-wives specifically, but whenever there was a phone call, a letter from the lawyers or a long court hearing, when I came home drained Estelle was always there to talk to, always there to help me. In an analysis of how good my relationship is with Estelle, all I can say is that those who are close to me and know precisely the emotional traumas I experienced can see the difference.

I love Estelle's approach to life. She is very mature for her age and I am sure that comes from being part of a famous family. There seem to be no inhibitions about her as a result of being involved with a well-known soccer player, and why should there be when she's related to such a renowned football star as Johan Cruyff? She also shows her maturity in her ability to come to terms with what is important to me, namely my two children from my Dutch marriage, and the two from my Italian marriage. It is good for me that she has a healthy relationship with all four of them. I love my kids and I'm very happy when I'm with them. I think about them all the time, I only desire what is best for them, and I want them to feel wanted by me, and I'm thankful that Estelle is coping so well with it all.

In fact I like all kids. I feel I can relate to them because I'm nothing more than a big kid at heart myself – and I'm not ashamed to admit it. I prefer children in many ways: they are more open and honest, they want to play and have fun. It's a pity that when they grow up so many of these facets disappear; when you become an adult you have to adhere to so many rules all the time – you can't do this, you can't do that. I'm very happy in the company of children – they keep me young and give me a youthful outlook, although they sometimes think I'm a bit strange! They seem to be very curious about me. Perhaps it's my physique, my appearance; very little children think I'm the bogeyman. If they're afraid of me, they'll look away when I look at them. That's honesty again: if they are scared, concerned or unsure, they'll let you know. Perhaps that's why I enjoy being a football player and mixing with football players. Maybe footballers are all children at heart.

Unfortunately football has changed over the years and has become more complex because of high financial rewards. No longer can you treat it like a game as I once did in the Jordaan. If you want to protect the money you earn from football you have to be far more professional off the field as well as on it, and if that means getting expert advice, then that is what needs to be done. I know from friends and colleagues, and from my own experiences, that when in Holland in the mid-1970s footballers began to earn substantial amounts of money, there were plenty of people around eager to take advantage of them – and I'm sure that's the case the world over. Footballers then got the reputation of being dumb, the sort of people anybody could steal from without them noticing – perhaps without them even *caring*. A vital lesson was learned from those mistakes. At first footballers knew little about contracts and business affairs, money-spinning and marketing, but now they know it's in their interests to know their rights, especially since the Bosman ruling.

Players are much more aware these days of their financial capabilities and earning power off the field as well as on it. They rarely put their own money into projects anymore and risk losing it; instead they lend their names to licensing contracts and the rewards have been tremendous. Footballers are no longer regarded as stupid. We now have the power to choose how we want to spend our lives, and if we need our own space we can insist on it. We can also pick and choose destinations, and play in a country where we feel at ease, which is another important and welcome aspect to the modern footballer.

There are times when you are sitting in restaurants or bars when you don't want people coming up to the table every minute asking for autographs because you are deep in conversation or wanting a bit of peace and quiet. There are times when you just want to walk down the street, mingle with the locals, take in the scenery. There are times when you have to say no and not offend anyone or have to deal with public repercussions at a later date. But to be honest, I very rarely say no, if at all. And if I ever do say no I feel so guilty about it afterwards, which makes me feel even worse than I did before. No one can be amiable and affable twenty-four hours a day, so I guess it's ridiculous to feel guilty, but I had less reason to feel that way in London anyway because I got far less hassle on the street. It was like being in paradise again, like being home in Amsterdam. I had my privacy and I could walk up the King's Road feeling at ease, feeling at 'home'. In London they might say, 'Hey Ruud, you okay?' but that's all.

In contrast, the Italians used to come up to you and squeeze your cheeks. They are too passionate as a people and they can't just let you go, they believe they own you, that you owe them something, maybe a pound of flesh. If I drove along the road in Italy minding my own business and the people in the car in front recognised me, there'd be all sorts of commotion. They'd all gather up in the back seat on their knees and stare at you, pointing, waving and shouting to make sure your attention was on them all the time. The same thing used to happen in Holland, but toned down because they'd consider it impolite to make a huge fuss. I have never felt more hunted than when I played for Milan. The supporters considered you to be accessible all the time. They wouldn't consider it a privilege to get your autograph, it is their right. They would beg you – 'Please, please, please, please!' – but say it insistently so that its real meaning was 'You *have* to give me your autograph!' It happened anywhere and everywhere, including away from the stadium and the training ground.

I clearly remember, during my first days in Milan, making the mistake of agreeing to a German TV crew's request to film me for a day in the city. We arrived at Il Duomo, the cathedral in Milan, and within minutes I was swamped by Milan fans shouting and screaming at the tops of their voices. In one way it was good to see their undiluted affection for the club and for myself, but the downside, as I quickly realised, was that never again would I be able to do the ordinary things in life – at least not in Milan. I couldn't go to the shops or walk down the street because the fans wouldn't let me. Some people might think that such adulation is worth attaining, even craving for, but it can deprive you of one of the most precious things in life: freedom, the freedom to do what you want to do whenever you want to do it. You must understand that I'm not criticising my celebrity status or people's interest in me. It's just that there are moments when, despite my public obligations and responsibilities, I really need my freedom.

10
LOVELY BOYS

'Lovely boys' was my term of endearment for the players at Stamford Bridge almost from the day I arrived. No one's really asked me why I call people I like 'lovely boys', so I'll tell you that it's a phrase I picked up when I was a little boy during the many evenings I sat at home watching television. One of my favourite programmes was from England, *It Ain't Half Hot, Mum*, and Windsor Davies, as I'm sure you know, always used that sergeant-major term for his men.

It came in very useful when I was appointed as Chelsea's player manager just short of a year since I'd first come to the club. I never imagined that I would be team coach, although I had entertained the thought as a possibility, but it came out of the blue when Glenn Hoddle was offered the job of national coach. I was delighted for him, although from a selfish point view I would have liked him to stick around at Chelsea – but how could he not have taken up such a post? My name was mentioned in the newspapers as Hoddle's successor, but I didn't place too much emphasis on the idea

145

until the club's chief executive Colin Hutchinson came to see me. He made it absolutely clear that the club wanted me to take the job. I told Colin I'd need time to give some serious thought to the matter, and he agreed.

The first thing that struck me was the added responsibility. With the role of the coach comes dealing with a huge array of characters – all of them diverse in nature, the necessity of personally generating an atmosphere where the players are willing to do and try out things for you, and the ability to solve problems on and off the field quickly and painlessly. That is the nature of the job. The coach is at the very centre of the whole machinery of putting a team together and getting it to play well; like the battery of a watch, it is from you that the team will get its motivation and derive its energy. For me the most important aspect of being a coach is to make a group of players function smoothly all the time with one another. The players don't necessarily have to like each other, but they must respect one another in terms of footballing ability. Coaches have many different modes of operation: some like to concentrate on motivation, others on tactics and strategy, but I just did it my way. I didn't do the job to any manual, nor did I copy the style of management of any of the coaches I played under during my career.

I certainly had to think very carefully about whether I wanted to take this on or not. While I was thinking it over, the Chelsea supporters helped me to make up my mind. I did it more for them than anything else. The last game of the 1995/6 season was at home against Blackburn Rovers, and it was Glenn Hoddle's farewell, but the fans were shouting my name, pleading for me to take the job. They were, of course, thanking Glenn for all he had done at the club, but at the same time urging me to replace him. I could see the placards the fans had written being held up in the crowd. They had taken me to their heart, and I was very moved by it all – and,

I must say, surprised. It wasn't a new experience for me, of course, but I certainly felt a different sort of bond between myself and the English fans – and I'm not just talking about Chelsea fans here, although naturally the bonding was more powerful there. It just seems to me that English people can relate more closely and easily to what a coach is trying to do.

The beauty – and sometimes the beast – of football is that everyone has an opinion. Every fan thinks he or she is better than the manager and could pick a successful team more consistently. Everyone is a coach: the milkman, the butcher, the pub owner – they all have their own ideas. I always used to be asked, 'Why didn't you play him?' or, 'Don't sell that player!' It was as if they were all coaching the team with me, and I liked it. I didn't mind it at all. Yes, okay, I confess there were times when I thought over the team I'd selected and wondered if I'd made the right decision. Maybe I should have played a particular player in a more suitable position, or maybe I picked the wrong shape altogether. But just because you analyse the decision after the event, there's no point in having regrets, and I didn't. Even if with the benefit of hindsight I made a mistake, I know I didn't pick the team originally with anything other than a win in mind, so it wasn't as if I should blame myself for sabotaging anything. I made my decisions purely in the interests of Chelsea Football Club, and sometimes, for instance, players can benefit from a rest, or their particular style might not be best suited to a particular opposition. There are a multitude of factors, all of which have to be taken into consideration.

Relationships between players and the coach are of vital importance. It wasn't so long before my elevation to coach that I was just another player in the dressing room, and making the transition wasn't easy. One minute I was used to the banter and the horseplay, then I had to distance myself from it to a certain extent. No longer could I sit at the back

147

of the team bus on the way to an away match, I had to sit up front with the 'Old Spice', old folk like Graham Rix, Gwyn Williams and Ossie the kit manager. It was difficult at the beginning, but got easier as time went by and everyone got accustomed to it. In fact, I adapted quicker than I thought I would. I know that some people used to say of me, 'Oh, he just strolls about!' But the players knew what to expect, and their understanding of what I wanted from them developed rapidly. I didn't have to remind them of their responsibilities every day.

But, don't forget, I was still a player, though I felt I needed to spend much more time on the bench in order to assess the way my team was playing. When all that adrenalin is rushing around your body on the pitch you can't help but concentrate on your own performance within the team framework, but as coach it was my job to watch the team because the team matters most. I had to withdraw myself totally from any other thoughts and act in a professional manner, systematically to be as effective as possible for the benefit of the team.

I also had to dismiss any bias or prejudice when judging my team – a coach cannot afford to let sentiment in any shape or form blur his assessment of individuals. When I first took over as coach it was fascinating to reassess all the players who had once been my team-mates. I had a strong feeling that there were some players who could do more – for example, in training or technical work – and some who would flourish in a different position. Frank Sinclair was a good example of that. Frank thought he had everything in the bag, he thought he was one of the best right-backs in the country. Fine – I have every respect for a player with plenty of confidence. But with all my experience in the game I knew he could give more and transform himself into a better player. Frank had a strong personality, and although he might not have thought I was wrong, he didn't accept my view readily.

My philosophy was simple: if the players did their job well, that was all I could ask of them; but if a player couldn't cope with the sort of level of effort and commitment I was demanding and I thought he was capable of it, then I was prepared to go into battle with him to get the best out of him. If that meant a row, so be it. I had plenty of rows with Frank Sinclair. I used to call him into my office and there were times when I would have a go at him. I was really hard on him: I told him he was wasting something precious inside of him, and that he'd be better off trying to coax it out. After a while I forced him to come in for half an hour before training every day, together with some of the other players, for extra technical work. He would do that with Andy Myers, Michael Duberry, Danny Granville, David Lee, Dan Petrescu and Luca Vialli. Especially for Frank I set up some extra technical workouts and insisted that he perform them. It took him a long time to accept it, but I told him, 'Frank, you must understand, those people who tap you on the shoulder and say you are doing well, they are the most dangerous people in your life, but those who tell you that you are doing something wrong, they are the genuine people who love you and are worried about you.' It's funny really that I said that then, in light of what later happened to me at Chelsea.

In the end, Frank realised all the work hadn't been for nothing because you could see the improvement in his game, and to watch a player make those strides forward is a source of great satisfaction for a coach. It's no coincidence that Jamaica want him for their squad in the World Cup Finals in France. In my view there is still room for more steps to be made – by the time I left the club he hadn't reached the heights he is capable of. Probably he doesn't realise himself how far he can go.

Dennis Wise is another case in point. When I was a player I played golf with Dennis and I had a good personal relationship with him. Then I was boss and I couldn't have friends in that sense in the team anymore, and the players gradually realised that I didn't have personal favourites in the team, that everyone was treated the same way. I was convinced that there was much more to Dennis as a player than his reputation at the time would lead you to believe. He was always labelled a tearaway, someone who kicked opponents, shouted and screamed, was generally undisciplined, something of a rogue. That was not the Dennis Wise I knew, and I wanted the player to emerge, and to achieve that I wanted more from him. I told him straight that there was only one way he was going to play in my team, and that was my way; if he didn't want to, he could sit on the bench beside me. So when he didn't conform to my plans for him, I left him out of the team. Naturally he was not very happy about it.

Dennis came to my home and we had a long chat about it over coffee. He had been so angry with me that until that day he hadn't spoken to me for a while. I didn't want to make him upset, of course, that's just the way it goes. Dennis Wise was a hero at Chelsea, but Luca Vialli was a superstar when he joined, and so was I, but we were out of the team on occasion as well. I had won the European Cup and many other honours, but you can't just say 'I'm a superstar' or 'I'm a hero' and expect a guaranteed place in the side – you have to do much more. I explained to Dennis precisely what I wanted from him. From that day Dennis Wise was a different person. He assumed the responsibility of captain with maturity and became much quieter and more authoritative as a result, much more like someone who wants to set an example to the rest of the players, not just wearing the armband for the sake of it. Dennis began to play one- or two-touch passes quickly and precisely, and became a vital player for us in midfield.

Scott Minto was another player with whom I had many rows in my office. But again, in the end the message got through and he has now got an FA Cup winners' medal and a good career at Benfica. The only one to benefit from all the arguments and hard work is the player. I didn't want Scott to leave the club, but he came to the end of his contract and took advantage of a free transfer. To emphasise there was no animosity, only mutual respect, he often came back to train with us when he was in London.

When I became coach at Chelsea, one of my first tasks was to buy my own lovely boys. My transfer targets were to forge the spine of the team, and that's why I wanted Luca Vialli, Roberto Di Matteo and Frank Leboeuf. There was no motive here other than to strengthen the team in the three major departments of defence, midfield and attack, but it always seemed that some criticism was aimed, especially when Gianfranco Zola became my fourth signing. The media immediately leapt on the fact that Italy and England were in the same World Cup qualifying group, and the stories and speculation started. Now that both countries have qualified, things have quietened down, but it's important to remember that I didn't assemble an Italian squad at Stamford Bridge, I assembled an international squad.

The first player I bought was Luca. I just rang him up because I knew he wanted to leave Juventus, and I did the same with Di Matteo and Leboeuf. My friend Ewald was very useful in alerting me to the availability of players. He works indirectly for a players' agent, and occasionally he tipped me off – he sent me a video of Frank Leboeuf, for instance, although I already knew about the two Italians. My main target was a defender, and I wanted a specialist sweeper, someone who reflected the way I played the game, the way I passed the ball, someone who saw the game being played from the back with a certain style. Glenn Hoddle wanted to achieve that when he bought me, and I wanted a player in my own image.

I must admit that until Ewald showed me that video of Leboeuf, I'd never heard of him. Ewald told me he was a reserve for the French national side and that no one outside France knew him very well. I was very happy he wasn't a high-profile player because I was able to go out and get him without starting a feeding frenzy. I noticed that he was in the French squad for Euro 96, and I know it's unkind on Frank, but I was just praying he wouldn't get a game so no one would spot him. Funnily enough, when I studied the video of Frank – an entire match he played for France – he didn't have a great game, but what I liked about him was his vision, the way he saw the game, and the fact that he was a good passer and tackler. In that video I felt he was sometimes biting into a tackle too early and was enticed out of the line too easily, but I wasn't too concerned by that – I felt it was easily rectified. You can't teach ability – whether a player possesses it or he doesn't – but you can coach someone to improve their positional play and their understanding of the game.

At the time I rang Frank to explain to him what I was seeking for Chelsea, I was working for the BBC as a match analyser for the European Championships. I used that position for research in my quest for new blood. I had three targets, I made three calls, and I got three players. I didn't have anybody else in mind and I didn't make any other calls. Zola came a couple of months later, and that was simply a case of him becoming available. It was extremely helpful during negotiations that we already had two Italians at Stamford Bridge, so naturally Zola had heard all about the club and our style of play. It was no surprise to me that he made an immediate impact when he arrived because he was in form and I expected him to fit in. Zola gave me just that extra bit of quality I was looking for; he is the kind of world-class player an opposition finds it very difficult to legislate for, a player in the mould of Marco van Basten or Diego Maradona.

There is little a coach needs to do with a Zola – to encourage him is to improve him. I believe that when a player has certain qualities quite often he will have small deficiencies, but it is always more worthwhile to concentrate on encouraging the qualities than to come down hard on the weaknesses. By all means work on them, yes, but get the priorities straight first. For instance, if I was to have said to Zola after a defeat at Blackburn when he missed an easy chance with a header, 'Right, we're going to give you fifty crosses and you are going to head the ball in and you are going to do it every day,' that's not really going to help him because heading the ball is not his speciality, and no matter how much we make him practise it we're not going to change his height. Of course I insisted he completed the routine heading exercises, but it's no use hammering him about it when we need to focus all energy on his sublime footballing skills. He scored a hat-trick in the very next game.

Winning the FA Cup having made four signings in my first season as coach was great, but it wasn't the complete job, far from it. That's why I went out and bought six new players before the start of the 1997/8 season. One of them was the Uruguayan Gustavo Poyet who I signed from Real Zaragoza, and he was making a major impact before he got injured. I always knew he'd play an important role for us, and when Chelsea lost him for the rest of the season it was a blow.

I bought Poyet and the rest of the players because I knew we needed to improve as a squad, and that required more quality, more strength in depth, throughout. A modern coach needs as many players as he can to meet the escalating requirements of the game. I knew already in my first year that I was short of players, that the squad was not strong enough to cope with injuries and suspensions. There were many occasions when we had to improvise far too much. In English football, with its tremendous pace and action, there are bound to be bookings, sendings-off and injuries during the course of a season, and a club has to have cover for every position. For an ambitious coach, cover means replacing quality with quality. I wanted twenty-two players each of whom was as important and valuable as the other. Some can accept such a policy, some can't. It's not easy for players to cope when they are not in the team, as I know only too well, but at Chelsea I tried my hardest to make them understand that everyone had a vital role to play, irrespective of whether they were picked regularly or not. The simple fact is that no one can play every game in an English season, and you also have to make allowances for fluctuations in fitness and form. Once the players relaxed with this philosophy, they bonded even more closely, and that was excellent for the atmosphere in the club and for team spirit.

At times, as I've said, I had rows with players, but I never had an argument with Luca Vialli. It might have come across in the media that we were at loggerheads, but as far as I'm concerned that just wasn't true. I had nothing but admiration for the way Luca acted at the start of his second season with the club, and he was a good example to all the young professionals at Chelsea, and the senior ones too. The facts about Vialli are that when he first arrived at the club he was injured all the time. He didn't look fully prepared for a game, and if you're not totally fit in England the game will find you out. But Luca was a big star, so it was difficult for me. At first I decided I would make an exception in the case of a superstar, but I was uneasy with it and knew it couldn't go on indefinitely.

One day I called the whole team together and told them that if a player didn't train properly during the week he couldn't play on the Saturday because he wouldn't be in the correct physical condition to do himself or the team justice. Once I set down that rule, there was no room for special consideration for anyone in the squad. By sheer coincidence, that was around the time that Zola became available, and I didn't hesitate to snap him up. Vialli was not in form – unfortunately for him he was suffering from his injuries – but Mark Hughes was playing out of his skin. My priority was the team, and I decided that my best striking partnership at the time was Hughes and Zola, and they were excellent together up front. I told Luca about my choice and I know he was hurt, and I didn't enjoy hurting him – I knew exactly how he felt. Later on I explained my thought processes to him in greater detail, but his pride in his abilities stood in the way of understanding, and I can't blame him for that. I emphasised, as always, that he still had an important and valuable role to play as a member of the Chelsea squad, and that he figured strongly in my plans for the club's European campaign. In fact, in Europe I was convinced he would be our main man.

There was endless speculation about whether or not Luca would leave the club, but I am certain he never wanted to go. Maybe in his mind he felt that was the only option to free himself from all the frustrations of the job, but he was happy in London, settled within the club, and enjoyed an excellent relationship with his team-mates. Nobody wanted him to go and everyone was delighted at how well he started the new season. He showed his determination by coming back to the fray with his injuries behind him, putting in extra work on the training field, and even by giving up smoking. That's a real professional attitude, and I was very pleased.

Among my other purchases was Tor Andre Flo who had an excellent reputation in international football in Norway. Perhaps he was frustrated too at not getting many starts at the beginning of the season, but only eleven men can go out onto that pitch. When you consider Chelsea were involved in Europe, the defence of the FA Cup, the Coca Cola Cup and the Premier League programme, you can see the need for many players of quality in the squad, and Flo was a valuable addition. Even with this extended squad there were times when we were stretched, and it's always annoying for a coach when, for example, you have a lot of players away on international duty. Of course it's a great honour for the player concerned and I would never forbid someone to play for his country in an important match, but a coach always worries about the condition of the player when he returns, how long he is going to be away, how far and where he is travelling, and how he's going to get back.

The only solution to this conflict between club and country is that every nation must play at the same time. It is a complex problem, but it should be a priority at FIFA that all internationals anywhere in the world are harmonised in terms of timing. It's a crazy situation, for instance, when Inter Milan can pay so much money for the world's most exciting talent, Ronaldo, only for him to go missing for so long for a series of international friendlies. One player doesn't make a team – Alan Shearer was the tournament's top scorer but England didn't win Euro 96; Ronaldo was top scorer in the Spanish league but Barcelona didn't win the title – but players of Ronaldo's quality are so rare that you can appreciate the unrest it's caused at the Italian club. To avoid this, at Chelsea, I wanted the whole team to be capable of scoring goals; to rely on just one, or even two, at the top level is courting trouble. If you rely on one player to lift the team and make it play attractive, potent football, what happens when he has an off day, leaves for an international tournament, or gets injured?

Football has changed dramatically over the years. It's become so quick and demanding, so much about a player's fitness, that it's impossible to play the same team all season. In the past a coach might have selected his best eleven and stuck with it, barring injuries and suspensions. Continuity within the team was a priority. But that's no longer the case – it's even difficult to play the same team in two successive games these days. Whether the game has improved as a result I don't know. I still enjoy it, but it has become more political, more commercial, and there is far more media involvement than perhaps is healthy.

I was very ambitious as a coach at Chelsea, but first I wanted the team to do well. If we scored a goal many thought I was too ultra-cool about it, but just because I don't react too much it doesn't mean I don't care. I have to do my job at the same time: I'm looking at the opposition and what they're doing as a result of the goal – you know there'll be some sort of reaction. They may step up a gear, or their coach may immediately try a change of tactics or personnel. I don't cheer when we are one or two goals up – only when we are three or four goals up. No matter what anybody might think, so long as it's a battle out there on the pitch I'm tensed up. I'm concentrating on the game and I might scream at the players to make sure they're still concentrating. You have to stay alert – the opposition will always wind themselves up and come straight back at you.

There's a challenge at every stage of the game. Often the fans will see a coach leaping up and down on the touchline, shouting at his players, but there's no need for that. They can't hear you anyway. At Chelsea, when I wanted to make an adjustment I preferred to wait two or three minutes for a player to come within range so that I didn't have to scream and let the whole ground know what I said. The opposition sometimes tried to be cute by sending a player over to eavesdrop, but here I had a big advantage: I always called over one of my Italian players and relayed the instructions in Italian. I remember once when we played Wimbledon, Vinny Jones got injured and was making his way to the bench. I wanted to use the opportunity to pass on some instructions so I called over Roberto Di Matteo and gave them to him in his native language. Afterwards I overheard Joe Kinnear asking Vinny about what I had said, and Vinny answered, 'I didn't understand a bloody thing – it was all in Italian!' I suppose later people thought I bought Ed de Goey just so I could speak to him in Dutch!

Normally I made major adjustments to the shape of the team at half-time when I could speak to all the players at once, but of course there are times in a match where every manager has to use his voice from the touchline – sometimes you can't wait until half-time to make a substitution or change tactics. First, though, I always tried to talk to that player during a break in play to explain to him precisely what I thought was going wrong, and how he could put it right. The player then gets a chance, but if it is still going wrong then, sorry, but it's an early bath. That individual will get another chance some other time, of course, but during a match the good of the team overrides all.

Team meetings prior to a match used not to last very long – typically around ten to fifteen minutes. If Chelsea were away from home I would hold the meeting in the hotel before leaving for the ground, if at home, then in the dressing room. The reason for this as I saw it was a matter of security, a means of ensuring that my team selection was kept away from the opposition to maintain the element of surprise. Rival managers seemed to be very interested in my choices, and some went to extraordinary lengths to find out. Before a match the kit man goes into the dressing room and lays out all the shirts with the names and numbers on the back, and then leaves. On one such occasion the coach of that day's opponents wandered into the Chelsea dressing room and was about to have a good look at the shirts when he was caught red-handed. He made some lame excuse before disappearing, but we all knew why he was there. And no, I'm not going to tell you who it was!

But spying in football is nothing new, it goes on all the time. Milan used to send spies to the training grounds of our opponents before virtually every match, so I know all about that sort of nonsense and it doesn't faze me. On another occasion a manager surreptitiously came to the Chelsea team hotel where we were training on a nearby pitch and was spotted peering through one of the windows. Someone also spotted the car, and we all knew who it belonged to. Fortunately we discovered all this before our training session, so we put out a phoney team on the pitch and started to practise some dummy manoeuvres and tactics. That manager might be shocked to discover that we knew all about his presence that day. He'll know who he is. We all had a big laugh about it later, after the match.

11

THE PRECIOUS
FA CUP

The penultimate week in October 1996 was a very strange one. Several bizarre things seemed to happen to me, I felt depressed and I did not get any sleep for a few nights. I had a series of weird dreams, and I would wake up in the morning and tell Estelle about them. I can't remember what they were about – you very rarely can – but I do remember waking up feeling nervous.

On the night of Tuesday, 22 October Chelsea were knocked out of the Coca Cola Cup by Bolton Wanderers on one of those frustrating nights when we were in control of the game yet somehow managed to lose it. On the way back from Burnden Park very early on Wednesday morning, we were sitting on the team bus playing cards as normal when Graham Rix received an unexpected call on his mobile phone. A journalist was on the other end of the line, and he told Graham the news that Matthew Harding, the club's financial saviour and vice-chairman, was dead. Graham Rix came to me pale-faced and said, 'This journalist guy's just told me that Matthew Harding died in a helicopter crash.' I couldn't believe it, and the news put us all in a confused state. We weren't happy to accept such news from the lips of a journalist alone, so we didn't tell the players anything about it. We decided to try to get it officially confirmed, and Graham and Gwyn Williams spent the rest of the journey back ringing as many people as possible to try to learn exactly what had happened. We felt terrible doing this, but we had to know. I told Graham to call me and let me know as soon as he heard any news, no matter what time it was.

When the story was eventually confirmed, my mind immediately flashed back to the events surrounding Paolo Mantovani's death while I was at Sampdoria, and further back to the deaths of Percy and Jerry Haatrecht in that horrific air crash in Surinam. I now knew why I had been feeling so terrible for the last few days – I wouldn't exactly call it a premonition, but there must be some explanation for it.

The mourners arrived early for Matthew Harding's funeral, among them Labour's deputy leader John Prescott, Glenn Hoddle and Ken Bates. It was a dark, dismal day at St Margaret's Church in Ditchling, a tiny village in East Sussex where Matthew had lived, but the weather reflected the mood of those gathered.

I didn't like this funeral at all; there was something about it that was not done well. Assembled inside that church were the people who loved Matthew the most, the people who had lived with him. His ex-wife Ruth and his girlfriend Vicky Jaramillo came together for the first time in that church, united in grief, so the main disappointment for me was that the vicar during his address didn't mention Vicky's name once. There was nothing about Matthew's life with her or about their daughter, Ella; instead the vicar spoke only of Ruth and her four children. Quite clearly the family didn't want to talk about one side of his life, and that is understandable, but for the vicar not to even mention Vicky's name was deplorable. She was sitting just in front of me throughout the service, and that young woman was in deep grief. Surely there was room for a kindly word, a little support, whether or not you disagreed with the way they had lived their lives? It was not the vicar's place at that funeral to be judgemental. He may have had his personal opinions on the matter, but in front of those in the church he should have expressed his sympathy on behalf of everyone; based on his Christian beliefs, based on everything that is decent, that girl deserved his support. The fact that Ruth and Vicky were in church to pay their respects to the man they loved showed that they were big enough to put aside whatever feelings they had. His omission gave the proceedings a bad atmosphere, as far as I was concerned.

After Matthew's death I went to church to pray for his soul. I'm not a religious person in the sense of being a Catholic, Methodist or Buddhist, but I believe in God and I go to church to talk to him because that's his house. Sometimes I read the Bible. My mother had one presented to her at school when she was young, and she gave it to me. I still have it and, remembering Father Robert's words, it does give me some comfort from time to time.

It was an emotional time for everyone at the football club, and we all found it very difficult to come to terms with this sudden loss, but there was a great bonding between the players as a result. What Sampdoria had felt unable to do after Mr Mantovani's funeral, Chelsea promptly went out and did. The following Saturday at Stamford Bridge we all had a quiet moment to ourselves in the dressing room before

163

going outside to lay a wreath at the foot of the new Matthew Harding Stand; we then joined hands around the goalmouth and the whole ground observed a minute's silence. And then we beat Tottenham Hotspur 3–1, just the way Matthew would have wanted it. But the best tribute to his memory would be to transform his dream of bringing silverware to the Bridge into a reality.

Abroad the FA Cup doesn't quite have the same magic as it does in this country, and even in my first season as a player with Chelsea it was impossible for me to capture fully its significance or its remarkably charismatic qualities. On the continent only the championship really counts, and although everyone watches the final from a distance, you cannot taste the enormity of it all.

In that first year Chelsea reached the semi-final stage and took on Manchester United. I scored with a close-range header to put us into the lead. The fans went wild, but I didn't really have a clue just how much it all meant to them. Naturally we would all have loved to reach the final, but the truth was we didn't have the quality to cope with a club as powerful as Manchester United. Even so, I felt we weren't all that far behind during the match – the cup is a great leveller – and with a bit of luck we might have progressed. Even Eric Cantona had to save one off the line right at the death. But we lost the match in the end and I went away from the game feeling unfortunate, and still not understanding the magnificent traditions and passions that attend the competition. Once we missed out on the final, the cup had little attraction for me and I didn't even tune in for the game between United and Liverpool. Later on I saw the goals, of course, but I didn't watch the whole match because I was so disappointed for Chelsea.

My second season at the club was different for many

reasons – quite naturally, of course, because now I was the coach. But once again the real significance of the tournament didn't hit me until the semi-final, even when we thrashed Liverpool 4–2. To all our fans that was something special, and to me it was important too, particularly the way we went about it. At the start we made some mistakes, and Chelsea were two goals down at half-time. I had to do something. Uppermost in my mind was to fashion something which would surprise the opposition in the second half, and for me that meant drastic changes because we were in a bad position, although I still felt that if we could create a few chances and change a number of aspects of our game we could get back into the match. It was perfectly clear and I gave the players their assignments – for instance, I wanted Di Matteo to mark John Barnes a lot closer to loosen his grip on the midfield – and told them that if they performed their tasks to the letter then we would win the tie. I remember being quite calm as I delivered those words. Sometimes a coach can go into a dressing room at half-time and without even saying a word, just by his demeanour, the expression on his face or even his attitude, the players can be filled with his positive vibes. The conviction I had that we would win transmitted itself to my players.

I've watched that game again on video and you can see in those TV pictures that I was relaxed and very quiet throughout that second half as the goals went in and we came back to win. As the game unfolded, so my conviction grew stronger. Later on I analysed how I had managed to change the course of the game. I knew I had to do something extreme, and the match perfectly illustrated my philosophy in football. If I'm 2–0 down, I'd rather lose 5–0 than mount a damage limitation exercise. I wanted my team to attack; I wanted them to create chances and put them away. As I said, at the time, sitting there in the dugout watching it all happen, it was no surprise to me, although the day after I recognised the fact that it was a sensational victory. The greatest aspect of that comeback against Liverpool was the pleasure I derived from seeing my players achieve. That always comes first as far as I'm concerned.

By the time we reached the semi-final the thrill of the FA Cup began to take me over. I also began to sense that the players knew they could win it. Sparky knew it. He'd been there before and won it three times, and he could sense it this time too. I had been at big clubs and I knew it. Dennis Wise was also convinced that this was Chelsea's year. The feeling permeated throughout the club, and even outside it: even friends of mine thought the cup had our name on it that year.

As the semi-final drew closer there was a pain in my stomach, a nervous pain, one that you can only get rid of by playing the game and getting it over and done with. Usually scouts are sent to watch the opposition before the match, but on this occasion I travelled down to Selhurst Park with Estelle and the Chelsea goalkeeping coach Eddie Niecszwyski, doubling as my note-taker, to watch Wimbledon play against Newcastle United. There I was, sitting in the stand and studying the way Wimbledon played. It felt strange because I'd always been more concerned about how my team played – ultimately it's their performance that dictates whether Chelsea win or lose. But on this occasion I felt I had to do it to confirm the validity of a number of tactics I was planning for the game. I had a feeling there was something I'd discover that would help Chelsea in the match.

As Joe Kinnear walked out to go to his dugout I saw him talking to one of his assistants. For some strange reason he looked up just at the split second I was looking at him. I waved at him. Wimbledon didn't have a particularly good game in the first half but they played better football than Newcastle, and then Faustino Asprilla scored a marvellous goal from a free kick. At half-time I had something to eat with Estelle and Eddie, and fifteen minutes into the second half I had seen what I had come to see and left.

The week before we had played our usual 5–3–2 formation; whatever numbers game you play it was Chelsea's style to have three central defenders and two wing-backs. But after watching Wimbledon I was convinced that the way to win the game was to change to a more conventional 4–4–2. I didn't have Doops (Michael Duberry) available, so I brought in Erland Johnsen to play centre-half alongside Frank Leboeuf with Scott Minto on the left and Frank Sinclair on the right. One thing I impressed upon the players was that I didn't subscribe to the widespread criticisms of Wimbledon's long-ball, hit-and-hope game. I didn't fall for any of that nonsense. The way Wimbledon play is perfectly planned; it is percentage football but everything centres on playing to their strengths. Their strikers run to precise positions and they have midfield players moving quickly forward to support. It is a mistake teams often make assuming they just kick the ball forward and hope for the best – it is far more methodical and clinical than that. Every time the ball is played to a certain position, there is always someone there in support to pick it up.

It was a lovely sunny April day at Highbury when I walked out of the tunnel to inspect the pitch. I breathed in the air and sensed we would win the match. In fact, we weren't in trouble once throughout the entire game. Zola scored a cracker, and when it was all over we were not just celebrating winning the FA Cup semi-final, we knew we would win at Wembley too. But of course we still had to win the match, and that's why, to get my preparation exactly right, I went with Graham Rix to watch the other FA Cup finalists, Middlesbrough, at Tottenham.

Before the FA Cup started I had discovered one or two

peculiar aspects of this marvellous competition. The players' pool, I found out, is a traditional pre-Cup Final method of pooling all the money made from interviews, sponsorships, the team song and all sorts of other commercial deals to be distributed at the discretion of the players between themselves, the staff and a number of chosen charities. It is a club's way of ensuring a fair distribution of the money generated by the FA Cup competition so that lesser known players and staff members right down to the tea lady get their fair share of the proceeds of success. It attracted a great deal of media criticism, with players being accused of greed, and this upset me a lot. I've seen cheques from the pool being signed over to hospitals and charities and other very worthy causes, so to say the players are like vultures is unjust and hurtful. I was proud of the fact that my players were happy to share their good fortune with others.

Nevertheless, I didn't participate in any of it. I have been involved in quite a few cup finals in my time and I know how best to prepare for them. It is best to be humble and not to be too big-headed, so I didn't take part in any of the peripheral activities like the team song for Wembley, and there was absolutely no way I was letting the BBC cameras onto the team bus before the final. The whole thing was a circus to me, and I wanted everyone to focus purely on winning the FA Cup. I insisted that everyone's attention in the days leading up to the final be centred on the game, and that everything had to be carefully co-ordinated prior to that. A team going into a final should have an aura about the way they behave which is transmitted to everyone around, an aura of invincibility if you like. Equally, they should always be respectful, fully aware of what their opponents for the day are capable of achieving but more concerned about what they themselves can achieve. The FA Cup Final was to be an historic moment for Chelsea Football Club, and I didn't want it to turn into a series of party pieces. Win the cup first, then have a party.

On the coach to Wembley my players were in a calm mood, playing cards, with nothing to distract them: no family, no journalists, no TV cameras. The nearer we got to the stadium the more you could feel the tension in the air. From the moment we boarded the coach and left the hotel grounds, that tension wound itself up with every yard we travelled. Then you could see the people, thousands of them screaming, shouting and waving their flags. The streets were packed, and by the time we reached the stadium I knew whether or not it was going to be a hostile day.

During the league programme, once the players were off the bus and into the stadium everyone did his own thing. I usually stayed in the locker room with Terry Byrne, Mike Banks and Ossie, just chatting. Sometimes we used to sing our favourite songs from the seventies – 'Tiger Feet' by Mudd, or a song by Showaddywaddy – but as soon as the players came in we stopped. There was no singing at Wembley, we just chatted a bit. I preferred to be in the locker room before a match because then you don't get distracted by anything going on outside, you just cocooned yourself away and got ready for the game in your own way and in your own time. It also gave me a chance to see how the players were behaving just before their big moment. The real work, though, had already been done. The team talk took place in the hotel before we left, and I had discussed Middlesbrough's strengths and weaknesses but, as always, I concentrated more on my own team. I believed we were the better of the two teams provided we played to our potential, and I said so to the players.

When we first walked out to inspect the Wembley turf we got a pretty hostile reception because the Middlesbrough fans were all packed in at the tunnel end. The first thing to greet us as we emerged was a sea of red and white and a cacophony of noise. That was the moment. That was the key moment. That was the time to look the fans in the eye, to see their anger and not be intimidated by it, so I looked into their faces and didn't flinch, which made them realise I was unfazed and in control.

I was told a week before the final that I was the first foreign coach to lead out a team at Wembley for a domestic cup final. Although later I reflected on that fact and was proud of it, at the time it was just another statistic and I had more important things to think about. The only thing that dominated my thoughts in those days leading up to the final was how to prepare the team in the best way for the battle ahead.

It was certainly a proud moment as I walked out of the Wembley tunnel at the head of my Chelsea team. It is a long and interesting walk to the centre touchline, and I enjoyed it very much. I didn't have long to wait before my players began to confirm my feelings that we would end the day as victors. Obviously there is a certain amount of luck involved when a team scores so early on in a game, but the way Roberto Di Matteo struck that shot into the back of the Middlesbrough net with forty-two seconds on the clock was beauty and professionalism personified. It spoke volumes about the determination of the team right from the word go. It would have been better for us to have scored in the final minute rather than the first, because Middlesbrough had the whole game to make amends and come back, but that is where our true strength lay on the day – our ability to contain so successfully for so long a team that had stepped up a gear from the opening minute.

At half-time I was very quiet in the dressing room. I just wanted my players to continue as they had been playing, and I simply told them that I wanted them to remain united and to continue to create chances. And that's what they did, and it was a wonderful back flick by Zola that allowed Eddie Newton to score Chelsea's second – and it was really nice to see Eddie get in among the goals.

So much fuss had been made during the build-up about whether or not Luca Vialli would play, or even if he would be on the bench or not. I was conscious too that this was his first FA Cup Final so I gave him a little run at the end of the match. After that second goal I could relax a bit and let Luca experience Wembley for himself, and I knew he was happy to be part of it. I was incredibly proud of my players. They had answered my faith in them in the best way possible – all season they had been willing to learn, hungry to improve, and this was a fitting result for all their hard work. It was not because of anything I had done; I had merely opened their eyes to the possibilities. It was their commitment that made it all work – instead of racing home after training they wanted to stay on and learn about the game, practise their techniques, eat the right foods. As I said, I was very proud of them when that final whistle went.

My magic moment was when Chelsea actually lifted the FA Cup. I've been so disappointed in other countries when that is the moment the broadcasters choose to cut their transmission and wander off to an advertisement break, but I was delighted to see that in England the lifting of the cup is the focal point of the final. When Dennis Wise held that cup aloft I was standing there on the pitch looking up, basking in the moment, so pleased for my players. In fact I was so engrossed that I didn't realise I was supposed to be up there on the balcony collecting my winners' medal. I was still standing on the pitch when I received a tap on the shoulder and a reminder. Then I raced up the steps to catch up.

All the tension had gone to be replaced by sheer enjoyment and total satisfaction. It was a triumph for everyone at the club, and of course the best of tributes to the memory of Matthew Harding. The only sad aspect was that he was not there to witness it, and that was a painful feeling for everyone connected with the club. I knew Matthew well, and he would have been over the moon at Chelsea's success.

The next stage was the celebrations – and how we celebrated. That night at the Waldorf Hotel just off The Strand was one big party. Dennis Wise went crazy, dancing, singing and making fun of everybody in the nicest possible way. Ken Bates was so proud of the FA Cup you could see it gleaming in his eyes every time he looked at it. This was what he had been waiting for, and he was like a big child in its presence. I made a speech in which I thanked everyone at the club, and then I announced that Estelle was pregnant. I hadn't told her I was going to say it there and then in front of all those people, but it just seemed to me the perfect moment. Estelle went as red in the face as a tomato, but everyone else went crazy. All the women gathered around her and asked her all sorts of questions – chat, chat, chat. Oh, she was so embarrassed. I asked her why she thought I'd done the wrong thing, and she told me, but it was all right really and later that night we all went out together with my Dutch friends to a bar discothèque.

The next morning we had to get up and go on an open-top bus to parade around the streets of London. There hadn't been much time for sleep, which is why in the photographs everyone is wearing sunglasses. When we first left the Waldorf in central London there wasn't much activity, but by the time we reached the Thames and then on into the Chelsea area you could see all the houses decked out in blue and white flags, and the closer we got to the town hall and Stamford Bridge the more packed out the streets were. I felt it was a pity there wasn't a bigger square outside the town hall, because so many ecstatic people were there.

Inside the town hall there was time to relax a bit, and I

had a long chat with Ted Troost, who had played an important role in Chelsea's build-up to the final: he conducted some relaxation therapy with the players, and also administered some treatment. A great deal depends on attitude when it comes to a big game like the FA Cup Final, and for that Ted was the man. I knew what he had done for me in my career, and I knew he'd have a beneficial effect on my lovely boys.

After all the excitement of the FA Cup and a long, hard season, it was time for an extended holiday. First Estelle and I went to Holland, and then on to Portugal with some friends, to play golf and chill out. I didn't see anyone from Holland, Italy or England the whole time I was out there, so I had a really good, quiet break – with a pregnant woman! There in Portugal was the time for all the flashbacks, for the personal sense of satisfaction to seep through.

My first European Cup success with AC Milan was an incredible experience for me, but this FA Cup victory equalled it. We stayed on at Wembley for what seemed like ages, listening to our fans singing the song 'Blue Day', and none of us wanted to leave. I didn't have to tell the players to go round for a second or third lap of honour because they did it themselves. They were determined to share Chelsea's success with our devoted fans and didn't want to leave the pitch. They had to finally, of course, because the Wembley groundsmen threatened to kick them out.

12
THE SACKING

The start of the 1997/8 season, my second in charge was always going to be the most exciting, the most exhilarating and challenging. In my first season nobody knew how far we could go and everyone was so grateful at winning the FA Cup, but I always knew the second year would be more testing, there'd be more pressure and so many people would think they knew better, because success changes a lot of people. My main concern was to see how attitudes changed and how everyone would cope with the pressure, the greater expectation level from the fans and the press, and a more focused opposition.

I started the season in the belief that we could win the championship, and my conviction was underlined when we played Manchester United in the Charity Shield, a match that proved to me we were capable of challenging for the title. We coped with the Premier League title holders then, and to be fair they coped with us. The game was decided on penalties but it was enough to convince me that we had the players to take the top team on.

Our first Premiership game was a defeat at Coventry. It was a set-back, but I still maintain it was the best game we've ever played! I still can't believe how we lost it. But it didn't worry me: I knew it was just one of those bizarre things that can happen from time to time in football. I was greatly encouraged by the excellent quality of our game, and I was sure it was only a matter of time before we started to collect points.

The expectations of the players had also risen and our opponents were making it more difficult for us. Those conditions combined meant it was not always possible to play such open football. You can imagine the instructions from the opposition coach: 'Chelsea are so good technically, you've got to close them down.' We had to find a new approach and we knew it wouldn't always be sexy football, it would need hard work and concentration.

We showed at Old Trafford that we were still on course. If it hadn't been for an offside goal we would have beaten them, but even so I was extremely proud of our performance. Bernard Lambourde played for the first time in midfield and did ever so well, but then we hit a period where we lost players like Gustavo Poyet, Eddie Newton, Andy Myers, Lambourde and Celestine Babayaro through injury, and like everybody in the Premiership we suffered some indifferent results. At times I had to prepare the team as best I could when we were without players through injury and suspension. My strength was that I could always change the strategy at half-time, and we used that to our advantage in a couple of games. Once again it was a new experience for the players and not all of them could cope with the fact that we had to win matches now that so many people thought we could challenge for the title.

Sometimes things go well, sometimes they don't, and it's always a learning process, but you can't expect in the season

176

after a successful one to win every game. There is bound to be a settling down period and that is when you see how people cope with the ups and downs football always brings. It happened even with Manchester United. On occasions Alex Ferguson was forced to switch his players around, and there were times when they didn't get the results they expected. Despite suspensions, injuries and illnesses, and even with a dip in form, Chelsea were still in second place come February and I was convinced that things were going to get easier as key players returned to the fray. I always believed I would get the team back on track.

Whenever Ken Bates or Colin Hutchinson asked me about my future at Chelsea there was only one answer: 'I'm staying.' There was was never any doubt in my mind that my commitment to the club was absolute, and although I had heard all the rumours about AC Milan, Feyenoord and the Dutch national job, that's all they were: no one approached me, and if they had taken any soundings they would know I was staying at Stamford Bridge. The world knew, I made it perfectly clear, emphatically so, when I was asked by the media just before Christmas and a couple of times after that that I wanted to sign an extension of my contract to the tune of two more years. Perhaps that weakened my bargaining position when it came to negotiations, but everyone at Chelsea knew it, from the chairman to his chief executive to my players.

Eventually Colin Hutchinson called me to a meeting in his offices at Stamford Bridge, nothing more than a routine meeting; he told me that he hadn't seen me for a long time and we should have a chat. 'Yes, okay, no problem,' I said, and we arranged the meeting for the afternoon of Thursday, 5 February, after training. When I drove from the Harlington training ground to the stadium there was nothing on my mind apart from thoughts of the team and what lay ahead.

At the beginning of the meeting there was a really good atmosphere between the two of us. We were chatting about all sorts of things connected with the future of the club. Colin told me about the latest progress with the council and the club's quest for planning permission to build a new stand, and we talked about the future of the players already at the club and the new players I planned to bring in for the next season. With the new rules in effect we were allowed to speak to players in England as well as those abroad from 1 January, and even sign them up, so planning had to be done well in advance. I was already very busy trying to bring Brian Laudrup from Glasgow Rangers to Chelsea. I had obtained his telephone number through a friend who had used his contacts in Scotland, and within the existing rules I was able to talk to him about Chelsea. I then mentioned to Colin that I had been alerted to an article that centre-half Jaap Stam had given in Holland. He had made it clear that he wished to leave PSV Eindhoven and he had stated that he wanted to sign for either Chelsea or Liverpool and was clearly eager to play in the Premiership. I rated him very highly and I wanted him badly. Everything was going fine in our talks, and even though it had been suggested that PSV might want something like £10 million for Stam, nothing was said that would make me think the club couldn't afford him.

Next on the agenda were discussions about staff changes, and here I was particularly keen to bring the club even closer to the élite on the continent. After our game against Manchester United in the Charity Shield all our kit was stolen. Surely that shouldn't be possible at a top Premiership club? Then when we turned up at Coventry we had the same colour kit as our opponents! I made the point that that mustn't happen anymore and we should examine the possibility of bringing in more professional help. It was also important to me that at the training ground we had no secretary, so calls

178

were coming through and being left on the answerphone or our physiotherapist, Mike Banks, was answering them. Now you cannot have the physio taking calls when he needs to be concentrating on co-ordinating the medical side of the club, and there are always X-rays or scans to be arranged as well as the routine treatment of the players. Put all that together, and Chelsea were still being run on an amateurish basis compared to the likes of Juventus or AC Milan, and that was part of our overall progress that had to be addressed. I suggested that we needed a secretary to co-ordinate the telephone calls at the training ground and Colin agreed. He sat there taking notes.

Throughout this entire meeting the vibes were good, everything was positive, the suggestions I was making seemed to be taken on board and there was no reason to think there was any hidden agenda. And if there was some sort of conspiracy to kick me out, why was he asking me about the changes I wanted for next year? Yet there are so many questions that remain unanswered for me after this meeting and it cannot simply be put down to coincidence.

All of a sudden, after all the discussions about the money being spent on the new stand and the transfer budgets for next season were concluded, Colin asked me: 'Okay, what will you want in your new contract?' I responded by telling him I was happy to sign for two more years. Then I mentioned a high figure. Yes, it was high, very high, but surely when you negotiate with anybody they would expect you to value yourself highly, and after all I had been reasonably successful, hadn't I? In response you would expect an offer to be low, and then the two parties talk some more and eventually reach a compromise somewhere in between. That happened all the time in my football career and I am sure it is the sort of thing that happens all the time in business.

179

There are two tables in Colin's office and we were sitting together at the round table, and as soon as I mentioned this figure, which has been well documented, Colin stood up and returned to his own desk where he looked at a book that would give him an idea of how much that would actually cost the club when you add on the tax and everything else, and he said: 'That's going to cost us a lot of money.' Well, I fully expected that he would come back and say, 'Let's talk about another figure,' or most likely he would ask for time to discuss these issues with his chairman Ken Bates, and then come back to me at a later date with a counter-offer. Instead of suggesting an alternative figure, he turned on me. As I said, there was a really good feeling between the two of us at the beginning, but now the atmosphere felt a little strange to me.

He said to me: 'I know you are a guy who is difficult to negotiate with from our previous times together.' But I found that rather baffling considering the nature of the two previous negotiations that we had had. The first time was when Colin and Glenn Hoddle came to see me in Milan in May 1995, and then I asked for around the same amount I was asking this time. They left the room together and came back after fifteen minutes to tell me they couldn't do it and would I accept this amount. I agreed, I signed and I came to Chelsea. The next time we talked was when I was offered a job as coach and it wasn't hard to negotiate with me then because I didn't ask for a single penny more to take on the extra responsibility. Instead, the club offered me bonuses that were success-related and I carried on on the same wage. I even remember Colin telling everyone a story that for the first few months after I arrived in London I didn't even bother to collect my wages and he had kept them in a drawer safely for me. Surely that doesn't sound like someone purely motivated by money, and of course I am not: because of all the success I have had in the past, money has not been a problem. I have always been paid what I am worth.

So it shocked me when Colin turned round and said: 'Of course, you must understand that if we don't come to an agreement we will have to look for a new coach.' Now that really stunned me. I thought I couldn't be surprised much more, but I was because then he said: 'I'd like you only to be a manager, not the player coach.' They didn't want me to be a player anymore, they wanted me to concentrate on management, and Colin said that they had learnt from their experiences with Glenn Hoddle how difficult it was to combine the two jobs of player and manager and that everything improved when he fully concentrated on the team. I listened to everything he said, but I told him I hadn't decided to give up playing and that was my decision. I thought to myself that this must be part of the negotiating ploy. I thought he was bluffing and I let it go.

I left Colin's office feeling bewildered. Something was not right, I could just sense it. Now, when I look back, there was clearly a different agenda. In my opinion something had already been decided before I even went into that room. Colin clearly wasn't interested in negotiating or even discussing these issues with me in the sense of trying to reach an agreement. Rather, he made the point that if we didn't reach agreement they would be getting a new coach and they would have to do it quickly. It is sheer nonsense to suggest that when I mentioned my figure I also said it was not negotiable. That just did not happen. I was waiting for them to say how much they wanted to pay me. I wanted to negotiate and I would have taken an acceptable amount, much less than the figure I asked for.

I can understand the ordinary man in the street being unable to come to terms with the sort of wages footballers now earn. Why should they? They are extraordinarily high, and the players at Chelsea, I am sure, are exceptionally well paid too. I know that some managers want to know the salaries of their players, but I don't, and that was one of the conditions of accepting the post as coach in the first place. I was not interested in whether a player earned more or less than me. Nor was I concerned about his transfer value. I was the coach and business affairs that involved contracts and transfer fees were the province of Colin Hutchinson. I harboured no jealousy or envy or concern about what another player was earning in comparison to my wages. But when I was asked how much I wanted many people might consider that in relation to what I have done for the club, in terms of recognition for my achievements, maybe it wasn't such an outrageous request. However, I must emphasise again that it was not a figure I expected them to agree to, and had they offered me less I would have accepted. There was no walk-out, there was no animosity, I just felt the whole ambience of the meeting had changed from being friendly to being aggressive and I couldn't quite understand why.

I went home and told the 'wife' what had happened. I said to Estelle: 'I'll be hearing from them in a few days.' I told her we would need to have more talks to settle my contract, and I knew, of course, that I would accept a lesser figure.

That weekend Chelsea didn't have a match, but I rang Colin on the Saturday because I wanted to discuss the situation regarding Laudrup and Stam. A friend of mine had called me to tip me off that PSV Eindhoven were ready to do business with Chelsea and I wanted to suggest to Colin that he rang Harry van Raay, the chairman at PSV, to open formal negotiations to buy Stam. I also wanted an update from Colin on the planned meeting with Laudrup on Monday, and I was told it was on schedule.

Monday, 9 February was a very interesting day. It started out without any concerns as I went off to Slough to play golf with Kevin Hitchcock, Franco Zola and Gwyn Williams. My golf had improved since my arrival in England and Gwyn and I were beating Franco and Kevin. As normal, Gwyn received many calls on his mobile phone, even while we were playing – club business has to go on, even on the golf course, and our priority at this time was the signing of Stam and Laudrup. Almost at the end of our eighteen-hole game Gwyn received a call cancelling the meeting later in the day with the Laudrups because Brian's wife, Mette, was ill and unable to fly. So there was no need to rush away; although Zola had to leave, the three of us stayed a little longer and had lunch in the clubhouse.

When I got back home I called the club to ask about Laudrup and I spoke to Colin. I had this intuitive feeling that all was not right. Colin said to me: 'Didn't Gwyn tell you that his wife is ill?' 'Yes,' I replied, and Colin said: 'I'll let you know when he's coming.' But these strange feelings that all was not right were still there and that's why I decided to ring Laudrup's wife. Mette confirmed she was ill and that the doctor had advised her it was better for her to stay at home than fly from Glasgow to London. I thought to myself, maybe I am being too suspicious.

On Tuesday we trained in the morning, and Wednesday was a day off. Thursday, 12 February was a day I won't forget in a hurry. All my negative thoughts over the previous few days had disappeared and I went into training in the morning as usual. I was very, very sharp that morning, I was in great shape during training – in fact I was almost on fire. Afterwards I went to my locker room as normal and took a shower. I knew Colin Hutchinson was at the training ground waiting to see me – he told me he would be there, and there was nothing unusual about that. He came to my office at the ground about midday and I asked him: 'Did you call PSV? And when is Laudrup coming down?'

'Before you hear this from somebody else you had better

hear it from me,' he said abruptly.

I listened.

'We've had talks with the board and the board have decided that we will not accept your demands. And the board have decided to look for a new coach.'

'What are you saying?' I was completely shocked. There was no way I wanted to leave Chelsea and you could imagine how I felt. I was a little angry to say the least. I said to Colin, 'All I've done for you and this club, this is all you have to say to me?' He told me it was about the money, that my demands were unacceptable, but I said, 'We didn't even negotiate, Colin.'

'It's the board,' he replied, lamely.

'I couldn't care less about the board, I was talking to you about this and you didn't even want to negotiate.'

'It's a board decision,' he repeated.

'Well, thank you very much for what's happened here,' and with that I stormed off. Yes, I walked out. I was angry. Very angry.

Colin Hutchinson had told me it was a board decision, it wasn't his. But he was the only person I spoke to. I wasn't content with that – I wanted to find Ken Bates. I know the club have criticised me for walking out on Colin, but I was humiliated by what he said, and I wanted to get out of the room. I didn't know whether he had finished or not, as far as I was concerned he had said plenty already and I couldn't imagine what else he had left to say. When I had cooled down enough to think clearly I remembered that what Colin had said is that they would find a new coach. I didn't imagine for one minute they had already found one. He wasn't explicit, but I thought it was logical that if they were going to look for a new coach it would take some time and that I would be there until the end of the season. Fine by me. If they wanted me out that was their decision, but I would still do a good job for myself, the team and my club. I would do my best and then finish at the end of the season. Okay, it was time to focus again on the team. But only a few minutes after the meeting with Hutchinson, I called Phil Smith, one of my representatives. 'Phil, there is something strange going on, I've just had this conversation with Colin and he has told me: "We want a new coach". I explained to Phil that it was a board decision about the new coach, and asked, 'What's going on?' He told me he'd been trying to get hold of *me*: only a few moments before he had received some phone calls from journalists – they had asked him to comment on my 'sacking'. One of them had even asked to buy the exclusive inside story! This was the first I'd heard about 'sacking'. All I'd heard from Hutchinson was that Chelsea would be looking for a new coach. Then Jon, Phil's brother, rang me and said: 'I've had a call and the talk in Italy is that Luca has become the new coach.' I was astounded. If they had only just told me they wanted a new coach, how could they have already appointed a new one? I thought to myself, What's he talking about? I asked him if he could confirm it for me.

Before I left the training ground I called Stamford Bridge and said I wanted to speak to Ken Bates, and that it was important. The secretary said he was in Drakes having lunch and had a tight schedule because a little later he was having a meeting with the council. I drove to the Bridge and parked my car and made another call from the car park. Again I asked to speak to Mr Bates but again I was told he was unavailable. But I was adamant I wanted to speak to him and told the secretary I would hang on the line. I must have been holding on for between fifteen and twenty minutes, trying to get through to him at Drakes. Eventually I was told to go to a meeting with him at 4.30 at the Conrad Hotel in Chelsea harbour. Just as they were telling me the time of this meeting I spotted Ken Bates with another guy in a black Porsche passing me! I got out of my car and switched off my mobile, and he looked at me, but he didn't do a thing. He didn't even stop to speak to me, and I just thought to myself, Bloody hell, he's in a hurry! I called Jon Smith again and told him what had happened, and repeated what I had said earlier: 'There are strange things going on here.'

'I've got some bad news for you, Ruud,' Jon replied. 'What I was told by a journalist is now on Teletext – you are sacked . . . immediately!'

It took me about ten minutes to drive from the Bridge to my flat in Cadogan Square. I rushed through the door and turned on Teletext and there it was: I was sacked immediately. I was astounded. It was just incredible.

I made a lot of calls and I discovered what had happened the day before with Brian Laudrup. I was told he was not coming because his wife was ill and now I discovered that he had been down in London having talks the day before I was sacked, and no one had told me about it. Now I understood why they didn't tell me: they didn't trust me anymore and they had been planning to sack me, and the answer I would love to know is how long had they been plotting that? They knew it was coming, I didn't. It all makes sense now – there was no point in my meeting the Laudrups when I wouldn't be the manager. Instead Laudrup went to lunch in London after being picked up at the airport by Gwyn Williams. Luca Vialli was present at a later meeting. How do I know all this? Well, Laudrup later called me to apologise for what had happened and he explained the details to me.

By now the flat was filling up with my friends and advisors. Jon Smith called in at Stamford Bridge but the club were arranging a press conference and we thought it might be at the Conrad. Our suspicion was that they wanted me at that press conference, but I wasn't going to go. Instead I wanted time to study a detailed press statement that had been released by the club. Just looking at that statement I knew it hadn't all been decided in one day, and that everything could not have been put in place overnight; in fact you would have to think it would be weeks rather that days. I was so angry. We immediately set about writing my own press release, but it was difficult: after all, I still hadn't *officially* been told I was fired.

The meeting with Ken Bates was rearranged for 6.30 at the Conrad Hotel after the club went ahead with their press conference with Bates, Hutchinson and Vialli at Drakes. The meeting was always going to be interesting to say the least. I had to prepare myself mentally to face Bates. I arrived at the hotel and Bates was accompanied by a guy I didn't recognise. When I asked who he was Bates told me he represented Chelsea Village.

'Can I have a talk alone with Mr Bates?' I asked.

We sat down together on a couch close to the restaurant. There was no private room – perhaps he suspected I might let off a bit of steam!

'Can you explain to me exactly what is happening?' I began.

'I don't know what is happening here,' Bates replied.

'Why didn't Chelsea make me an offer?' I countered.

'I don't know – I have every faith in my employees and Colin Hutchinson deals with football matters and he talked to you, I trust him.'

'Why didn't you check with your employee to ask him what was going on?'

'We have made a decision and it is a board decision.'

There was no doubt in my mind that Ken Bates was hiding behind Colin Hutchinson. He was just listening to me – he wasn't offering me any answers. I was not rude to him but I was not happy about what had happened, and he knew it. He told me he wasn't at the meeting when we talked about matters and he left it to Colin Hutchinson.

They had already planned everything behind my back. I was bitterly disappointed about what had happened to me and I wanted Ken Bates to tell me why. I never got an answer; I know I never shall. I was in shock. I am totally amazed at the way I have been treated by the club I have given so much to. I had gone to this meeting in search of answers and I wasn't going to get them. Finally I turned round to Bates and told him, 'Don't worry, I am very confident about myself and everything will come straight again for me one day. Maybe we shall meet each other again – when that happens don't forget me.' I then left with a final few words: 'Give my regards to Suzannah.' As I got up to go he took a letter out of his pocket and handed it to me. I went outside the hotel and got into my car, where I read that letter. I was sacked, and I was not even allowed access to the training ground.

The worst aspect of all this was my big disappointment with some of those people around me. I'm not angry with Luca, I am not angry with any of the players, I am angry and extremely disappointed with some of those people I had around me. The next day I had my own press conference arranged by The First Artist Corporation in the International Sportsman's Club in Kensington. It seemed every TV and print journalist in London was there. I'd had a sleepless night, but I was ready to put my side of the story. I sat in front of the barrage of cameras and talked solidly for twenty minutes. The news was carried live by Sky and the BBC. Every time I went to scratch my nose a hundred flash bulbs went off. Afterwards I made sure I spoke to every single journalist who wanted to speak to me. I know how much the club have criticised me for the things I said when I had my own press conference the next day, but all I did was put the record straight from my point of view, and if you noticed I never made it personal, never criticised anybody, never attacked anybody, never blamed anybody. But they attacked me and they made it personal against me. There's a gentleman's agreement in football – at least there certainly has been wherever I have played, and that has been at some big clubs – and in my view it exists in England.

Yes, we may have had a difference of opinion, but a 'Thank you for what you've done' from the club would have been more appropriate than a kick in the goolies. And that's what I got from certain people. Those that I once called colleagues. I won't even demean myself by responding to some of the criticism. All I will say is that I have read some crazy things and cannot believe they have been said.

I would also say what comes around goes around. It's been a good lesson in life for me. I shouldn't have been surprised by what has happened because they always say that football shouldn't surprise you. But look at some of the great players, truly some of the world's top ones like Maradona, Cruyff, Beckenbauer, Bobby Moore, Kevin Keegan; they have always been riddled with problems. You would never find a colleague, a friend, with a bad word against them. Even if they thought it, they wouldn't say it, certainly not in public and definitely not to the papers. That is the gentleman's agreement that exists in football and that is why I am really, really astounded about what's happened at Chelsea. It has been out of order. I have suffered a lot of grief, experienced a lot of anger and said many things, but I never singled out anybody because I still say that I have experienced a lot of good times and a lot of good things at Chelsea and I owe so much to many people at the club, although I would also say there are quite a few people at Chelsea who owe a lot to me.

I want to remember the good times. I want to learn from the bad ones. Loyalty in football is transient and that's why when I spoke to a lot of the players I told them they must carry on and do their best for themselves, the club and their new manager. I couldn't see the Coca Cola Cup semi-final second-leg game against Arsenal on 18 February on TV in Holland, which Chelsea won 3–1 on the night and 4–3 on aggregate, but I talked to the players beforehand by phone and told them that to expect loyalty in football is to believe you are living in Utopia, and you're not. I appreciated their concern for me and all the things that have happened to me, and I thank them for that, but I told them they had to think of their own careers and what they can achieve at Chelsea and then in the World Cup in France. They have done their best and they can go still further. I was so happy that they beat Arsenal and I want them to win the Coca Cola Cup – they are still my players.

No, I didn't receive a call from Vialli. But I understand that in football, 'the king is dead, long live the king' and I wish him well and I wish the club well. I want them to continue to do well, in fact to do better. I have experienced changes like this before and I will still share in the team's success because I am still being paid until my contract runs out, and that includes my bonuses for success. But that is like the dessert; the main course is the trophy or the title. I brought the team to the semi-finals and I knew they would get to another Wembley final. I knew already they would be fired up to beat Arsenal. It was no surprise to me – it would have been a surprise if they hadn't won. The material is there, the right players and the talent. I never said to anybody that I thought we could win the championship this season, but inside I believed it, and if it doesn't happen this season it will happen the next. There were more good players I was bringing to the club.

Perhaps the biggest lesson I have learnt is that when I get my next job in coaching I will want my own men around me. There is a tendency with those people with whom you have surrounded yourself to become harder as a person and not to trust anybody anymore. I am determined that won't happen to me. I won't let them change me.

I know everyone has one question to ask me, and that is, What do I feel about Ken Bates? That is hard to answer. In truth I don't have any real feelings. I don't have anything for him. I never had a real relationship with him and he can do what he wants to do with his club, and that is precisely what he did with me. My question to him about why I was sacked was never properly answered, but I am not fooled by Ken Bates hiding behind Colin Hutchinson. I wasn't impressed when he said he didn't know what was going on when of course he knew about everything – Bates is the boss of bosses at the Bridge, and he sacked me.

So, what was the real reason? Everybody knows it wasn't about money. It's pretty transparent that that was the big stick with which they hoped to beat me, and it failed. Because it didn't work they had to come up with another reason, and they were plentiful. But no one believed it was about money when a few days after they sacked me they put the season ticket prices up by forty per cent. If they were saying I'm greedy, what does that say about them? The club is already the most expensive in football, so I am sure the supporters will have their own answers for that one.

It didn't take the club long to change tack from greed to other reasons. Colin Hutchinson said on BBC's *Grandstand* Football Focus that I had 'lost it'. But everyone knows that is not true also. From managers to chairmen to people in the street, anyone who had seen me knows that I had not lost it. Then I was accused of not being committed, not putting in enough hours like the British managers do. But that is sheer nonsense because we had a different structure in place, and the club knew it. When they asked me to become coach – and let's not forget they came to me, not the other way around –

I said okay, provided we do it in the way that can enable me to carry on playing and concentrating solely on the team. Those were the conditions I set down as a prerequisite for taking the job – it was only when they were met that I accepted the job. It was a simple but effective strategy. I could not be in the office dealing with paperwork and calls or the business affairs of the club if I was to be a player training every day and concentrating on the coaching. I needed people around me to do all the peripheral work, and that was all put into place. I also made it clear at the time that I would separate my private life from my football life and they agreed. It certainly worked well enough to win the FA Cup in my very first season as coach.

No one will ever be able to take away from me the elation of winning the FA Cup. It will live with me for ever, it will be the most overpowering image of my time in English football. I still remember when I called down from the stands to Ken Bates on the Wembley pitch and personally put the FA Cup in his hands. I didn't hear anyone at that time make any sort of suggestion that I was doing the job in the wrong way or that I wasn't spending enough time at the club, or anything else for that matter. I also remember that the chairman gave me a kiss on the cheek when I went up to collect my medal. He also gave me a big hug. He wanted to give me his lucky leprechaun too. I thought it was a joke and I laughed, but I didn't refuse it. These are wonderful memories for me: everyone was so happy and there was not a murmur of discontent. Nothing had changed apart from improvements I had made to the team and my conviction that we would do even better. Strange, then, that the board had lost faith. I can only draw the conclusion that they were trying to find some reason to get rid of me.

A manager can only be judged on the team he puts out on the field and on results – nothing else. If a manager gets those

Arriving in Sicily to prepare for the 1990 World Cup Finals. There's no escaping the media, recorders and notebooks from the start to the finish

Sports psychologist Ted Troost, who has treated and advised me at crucial stages throughout my career

At Eindhoven with Marcel Vaenburg

Left: Dutch resident, Welshman Barry Hughes, who recommended me as a young player to Arsenal and Spurs. He was my first coach in Holland

Facing page: In action for PSV Eindhoven at Feyenoord Stadium

With PSV Eindhoven president, Jacques Ruts, saying an emotional farewell to PSV fans before my departure to AC Milan

Enjoying my debut for Chelsea. I started in the Premiership as sweeper, but Glen Hoddle soon asked me to play in midfield and I was happy to oblige him

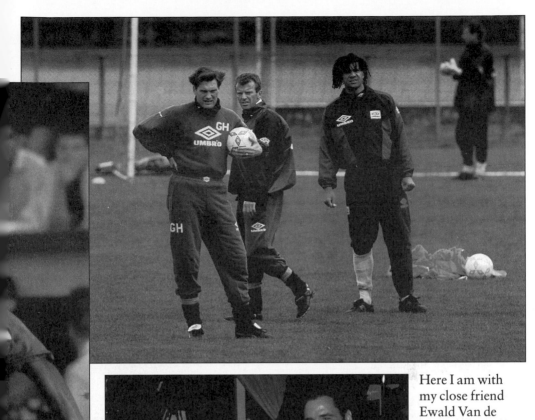

Here I am with my close friend Ewald Van de Bogt. This is a significant moment; he rescued me from my lonely existence in London by inviting me to Amsterdam for New Years Eve

Again, with another close friend, Frank Rijkaard, at the restaurant where I first met Estelle

Left: Ewald's wife to my left as I attempt to blow out the candles on my thirty-fifth birthday cake

Below: Golf is my passion and I'm improving all the time. In this photo I'm with the Dutch team in Sweden for the European Championships

Above: Estelle looks radiant at seven months pregnant. We're with my mum and her best friend Joke

Left: I preferred our private sessions than being on stage with the group *Revelation Time*

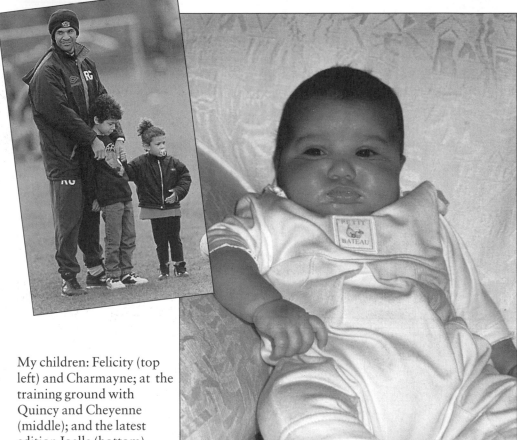

My children: Felicity (top left) and Charmayne; at the training ground with Quincy and Cheyenne (middle); and the latest edition Joelle (bottom)

results then he is doing the job correctly, however he might choose to go about it.

When I got home to Holland, every day I was getting calls; so many people were bewildered and my close friends and family felt so sorry for me. Everyone was upset about what had happened, even the people I met in the street, the ordinary people who kept on telling me: 'You will get a big club and there will be a club who will appreciate you.' It's impossible, however, to take away the pain even though I appreciated all the comforting words. It's also reassuring that they seem to understand what has gone on, that Chelsea have been searching for excuses but there is still no satisfactory explanation. Even outsiders can see there has been an injustice, that it was illogical to sack the manager of a team who were second in the Premiership, in the last eight in Europe and in the semi-final of one cup competition, having already won the FA Cup.

I've been around for many years now but I can never recall anywhere a coach being pushed out of a club at such a critical stage of a season. I've never heard of that, I still cannot understand it. All right, if they decided to get rid of me, for whatever reason, it would have been far more sensible to have done it at the end of the season. They could even have come to me and told me that. Even when there were hints that they wanted to change the coach I would have accepted it and carried on to the end of the season and done my best for that football club. There was something I could see within my grasp, something important still to be achieved, and I would willingly have carried on to complete the job. Chelsea was a diamond in my hand, a rough diamond that I had been shaping, and I was halfway through that job when they took it away from me.

Could it be that within just one week in the Premier League they lost their chance of the championship? I never lost two League games in a row in the 1997/8 season, but that is what happened when I left. I expected Chelsea to finish in first place, but I would have been content to qualify for the Champions League in second place.

I leave Chelsea with my head held high and I am happy for myself that I have achieved such success. I leave the club wishing the players all the best and hoping they do even better, and I have told a lot of them that we will meet each other again, and I hope that we do!

It has been difficult for me to comprehend what has happened. I have spoken to Estelle and reminded her about how we first met and what I told her then about all the jealousy, the hurt, the anger and the pain, and how hard it is to live through all of this sometimes. I am sure she didn't understand at the time – it must have been very difficult for her – but I think she understands it all the more now. Estelle has been a tower of strength, a great comfort to me, particularly in the first week. I spent that first week at home in Holland with Estelle and the baby and didn't have the inclination to do anything, not even to train. It was funny really because Estelle had warned me many times when we were in London – and she made the point about the friends I had made there – that I was too open with people, too trusting. You know women have a sixth sense about these things. Well, I can't argue with her now, can I? I told her that she was right and perhaps I should have listened a little more closely to what she had said. Estelle always told me to be careful and not to put my faith in the people around me.

Sometimes in life you have to discover these things for yourself. Unfortunately the way I found out is a little bit extreme. It's been a very good lesson, but I could have discovered it in an easier way. But I am a big boy and I've had problems at other clubs and I've come back. If nothing else, I'm a fighter. I'm at my best when my back is up against the wall.

I know what they have been saying about me, that I am arrogant or aloof, and I can imagine why some people might think that. The hardest thing sometimes is to learn to say 'No' to all the people who want you do something for them. You can't imagine how many people want to invite me here or there and promise me all sorts of things if I go with them because they want to be seen with someone who is famous – but I can't do it all. Many people will accept it, but there are some out there who are bloodsuckers, who want to eat away at you and take from you. Those people I turned down, those I've not socialised with or encouraged or put on some kind of act for, I've no doubt that they have called me arrogant and aloof. But the people who know me really well, the people I love, respect and take into my confidence, to them I am very open, perhaps too open. I'm not open or accommodating to those who just like to be seen with me for their own egos, who want to socialise with me for their own purposes – these are the shadow people who want to be behind you or beside you wherever you go.

The most difficult thing for a footballer, particularly a well-known one, is to say 'No'. I don't want to do it, but if I just kept on saying 'Yes' every day I would have a full diary: I would be out on the town every night, I would be at every show; I was invited everywhere. They wanted me to appear on *A Question of Sport*, on chat shows and all sorts of television programmes, but I would always say 'No'. I would always say 'Yes' if it was to involve kids. I appeared on a Walt Disney programme and I did an early-morning phone-in on *Live and Kickin'*. I would do anything for kids.

I've thought for many hours about my time at Chelsea, the good times and the bad times, my mistakes and my successes, how I went about the job. What can I learn from all of these things? No matter how much I think about it I still find it impossible to believe I was sacked because of any of

195

the issues that have already been raised; there has to be something more to it, something yet to emerge. I have received a number of telephone calls from people in the English football world; managers, directors, journalists and players from various teams who believe they know the answer. These calls have come from the kind of people who might just be right, but it is only their opinion. They have told me that I was getting too much attention at Chelsea Football Club. Chelsea was becoming Gullit – that's what people have told me. They might be right, but I don't know if that is true. I don't understand if it *is* true. I don't have feelings of jealousy and I find it hard to understand how people can be envious of someone else. If somebody has something I haven't got I can be happy for them, not envious of it. That is respectful. Equally it is possible to admire things in other people. Envy? I just don't understand it. But I have also been told that perhaps it was the same situation with Matthew Harding: the scenario developed and people have told me that Harding had become too popular; even after his death they would sing his name.

If that is the case, it is pitiful and I shouldn't be regretting the fact that I have been sacked. If that is the case I should be glad I am gone. I wouldn't want to work in an atmosphere like that any longer and I comfort myself with that thought.

13
REFLECTIONS ON CHELSEA

My desire at Chelsea was to create one of the best club sides in the world, and my departure hasn't altered my opinion that that can be achieved. The foundations have been set, the players are there, and new ones are arriving for next season.

If you stop and think about how trophy-winning heights are reached then there is only one logical conclusion, and that is that you need a massive squad of players and it has to be quality not simply quantity.

Again, logically there isn't room all the time for all the best players, there has to be a rotation system. It happens on the continent with the biggest clubs and it happens here with Manchester United. But for some reason no one made a big deal out of how Alex Ferguson went about rotating his players at Manchester United.

I noticed, not long after I had left Stamford Bridge, that

Ferguson brought in players like Jordi Cruyff and rested other players even though it was a vital Premiership game. I used the rotation system more for the Coca Cola Cup than anything else, and I did it for a reason: to give as many players a taste of the first team so that it's not such a huge surprise when they are needed for important games.

Gone are the times when a top club could have a first-team squad of sixteen players and the team virtually picked itself with the best eleven and five in reserve. Everything in football has drastically changed over the years: the Bosman ruling has allowed players free movement, and at the top end of the market hugely increased their bargaining power in terms of wages. Then there is the power of television and the saturation levels in the media. And sponsors are becoming more dictatorial, ploughing huge sums into football clubs. It has all created a change in attitudes, and to live with it all there has to be a change in direction about how clubs are managed. Pressure for success has been magnified to almost intolerable levels, and quite clearly players cannot play constantly under such pressure. All around the world the leading clubs are coming to terms with these changes, and I had to bring them in at Chelsea.

Let's face it, Chelsea was not in that situation when I arrived. They were rarely mentioned as a top club in England, let alone in Europe or indeed the world. One of my first tasks was to change the mentality and to make everyone perceive Chelsea as a top club, and that was the only way to take them forward. In my first year as coach the team focused more on the FA Cup than the Premiership because we were not strong enough in the League. When I started my second year I was determined to focus on the Premiership and the European Cup Winners' Cup. The Champions League has become the number one tournament, but everyone has aspirations for the top. That is where the big money lies and that is where the top players want to perform. Premiership football is totally different to Cup games, and right from the start of the season I made my point to the players: 'You are not going to win the League by beating Manchester United or Liverpool, but you will do if you beat the so-called lower teams.' I brought a number of players to Chelsea in the summer, and if I couldn't win the League I would have settled for the second place that brings qualification for the Champions League.

As I planned all the competitions the players would have to compete in, it was quite clear that I had to have the players to rotate, to ensure that they were kept fresh. Some players didn't like the system at first, but they got used to it and came to appreciate it when it brought good results. There were, of course, some insurmountable problems because some people didn't understand and refused to appreciate how it worked. And my suspicion was that those people were outside the dressing room, maybe trying to influence what happened inside. For example, I heard some criticism this season that I should have played Zola and Wise at Everton. We went to Goodison Park with a chance of closing in on Manchester United at the top. But Zola was not in good shape and Dennis Wise himself asked me not to put him on the bench. We sat on the coach talking while the rest of the players went into the ground, and Dennis was concerned with his toe problem – it just wouldn't heal. He had played with it for a long time and the medical staff were very supportive. Dennis felt it best not to play and I agreed with him – it was his decision. Unfortunately we lost at Everton 3–1 and I know there was criticism outside that Wise and Zola should have played. Zola was always going to be a difficult decision for me; I knew that the Italian media would be asking searching questions if I left him out. Why not? That's their job, and I have no problem with that. It was obvious that if I had left out an English player the Italian media wouldn't have cared less, but when I leave out an Italian they want to know why. No one questioned me too much about Dennis Wise not playing. It was a very, very important stage of the season and Dennis had been playing for long periods, even without training. That went against my principles. I prefer players to be in good physical shape before I pick them for the team, but I made an exception for Dennis and that shows you how valuable I considered him.

I had a good relationship with my players and it was sad that I had to leave them, particularly as I was unable to go to the training ground to thank them all personally and had to make do taking their calls on my mobile phone. Dennis Wise was a perfect example of a player who at first couldn't come to terms with my ideas and who then appreciated them more than anyone. At first he was used to playing in an average team, but now he's playing in a much better team he has become better himself. He has been producing such quality performances, it always baffled me that he was ignored by England. Dennis had to come to terms with my edict that if you didn't play well there was always another player who would take your place, and when I left him out he was unhappy about it. But I've always felt that there comes a time when there is no other way. At first I tried to talk to players to encourage them, but there are times when you need to stimulate them by leaving them out of the team.

As for Zola, I brought him to the club and I had faith in him, but I also had to leave him out this season. Sometimes it is impossible to perform every single game to your maximum, and Zola had a formidable first season and no one was more pleased than me when he was voted Footballer of the Year. But it happens to the greatest players in the world – you can lose form. Even in this country you can analyse the highs and lows of goalscorers comparable to

Zola. Andy Cole was stuck in a depressing sequence of form when he just couldn't score, but look how he came back. Alan Shearer went for a long, long spell before the European Championships without a goal, and there were even some who lost faith in him.

Every player can lose his form at times, especially strikers, and it can be harder for them when their only value is judged by their goals. There are any number of reasons that can contribute to such dips in form, ranging from injury problems to suspensions and personal worries. I must admit I don't know what was behind Zola's problem. I just put it down to simply having one of those spells, and I was convinced he would come out of it, and no one wanted him to do that more than I did. Of course, with a player of his reputation it is harder for him to take. I kept faith with him for as long as I could, but there had to come a time when another player got his chance, and there were plenty of options: Flo, Hughes or Vialli.

It was a difficult decision, because when Shearer doesn't play for Newcastle it is not Newcastle anymore, and it is the same at Chelsea – we are less powerful in attack if Zola is not functioning at his best. There was always a debate about where best to play him, but it soon became apparent that his best position was up front as a second striker. He is able to play on his intuition – sometimes you can't coach such amazing ability, it just happens. My aim was to try to stimulate that intuition again, and I felt the ideal way to do that was to play him in his best position.

Confidence is always a major factor, and I was fully aware when I dropped him that there was a danger of it affecting his confidence. I didn't want to leave him out because I was sure it was only a matter of time before he returned to his best. However, you can let it go for two or three games as a manager, but after five or six there comes a time to do something about it. I knew he was important to the team but I hoped that by leaving him out it would stimulate him so that when he returned he would be more fired up. I'm not saying this was Zola's attitude, but I know from my own experiences the players are always reluctant to blame themselves; they can find a multitude of excuses, pointing the finger everywhere except at themselves. It is typical to blame someone else, but the best players can be self-analytical.

Zola scored a hat-trick against Derby and then went into a period without scoring a goal. Sometimes such a dip is difficult to come out of, but I don't blame the player, and equally it can have nothing to do with the coach. The player tries his best but it just doesn't come off, and there can be no apparent reason for it. Putting a player on the bench can make him angry and that can be stimulation in itself. Dennis Wise showed me what he can do, he proved me wrong, and I was delighted, and I wanted Zola to prove me wrong too. I'd love to do it the nice way all the time, but it's a difficult job and I've discovered that coaching and management is not about popularity contests, it is all about doing what is right for the team.

Tor Andre Flo was a player who had his critics, I am sure, but I was very happy with him. I was aware of a number of clubs wanting to sign him last year and I had been following him even before I became coach. Through my own sources I was sent videotapes of him, and I also saw him playing a Champions League tie against PSV Eindhoven. I never believed he would be an instant success because it was a very big change for him coming from Norway to a club like Chelsea. But he was making steady progress and I was pleased with that. I called him 'Pistol Pete' because he was like a pistol the way he scored his goals with so much ease. He has the capacity to be a great player, but he still has an awful lot to learn about English football and the only way to do that is by training at Chelsea and playing games with us. Slowly, his talent will emerge, and I am convinced he will be a good player for Chelsea in the future. For the price that Chelsea paid he is a bargain, and it is only a matter of time before the Chelsea fans see the best of him.

Gustavo Poyet was a very important player for me and the team. Chelsea knew about him, having played against Real Zaragoza in the European Cup, but I had heard from my own sources about him and it was coincidental that the club mentioned him to me at the same time that I had been sent tapes of him. Again, it was a good deal for the club considering he came on a free transfer. The Uruguayan was a key influence in midfield and it was a big blow that he had sustained such a serious injury in training so early in the season. He had settled into the team quickly, and while he was influential on the ground he was also a big guy who could score many goals with his head.

We had big hopes for the Nigerian Celestine Babayaro, who I bought from Anderlecht, but again he was injured even before the season started. We didn't have somebody on the left side, so we bought Graham Le Saux. I've been charmed by Graham – he is an interesting character and a very fine footballer. But sometimes he plays too much on his anger. He has a lot of qualities and I believe in him, but he can become irritated far too easily and that can be a huge disadvantage at times. If he can calm down within himself a little bit more he will become an even better player.

Mark Hughes and Steve Clarke proved very important senior players. Their experience was vital, but they also have charisma. I had already offered Steve Clarke a position in the back-room staff when his career finished. He is a really nice guy and very important to the team. He is very quiet, but when he talks everybody listens. He doesn't say too much, but what he has to say is worth listening to. It is the same with Mark Hughes. When Mark says something the other players listen very carefully. These players are natural leaders, and at times I have made them captain of the team.

Frank Leboeuf is another very influential player. When I was looking for a defender the main attribute I wanted was that he would be good on the ball, and those were the qualities I spotted in Frank when I saw him playing for the French national team and for Strasbourg. He became very important to my strategy and it was always noticeable there was something missing if he was injured or suspended. Frank is a very passionate player, he wants to be involved in everything. The first thing I had to do when we signed him was to calm him down. I wanted him to play more on his skill than on his temperament, and he is a quality player who organises defence very well. In England it is normal to have a big, strong centre-half who tackles well rather than someone who plays the ball out of defence with long-range, accurate passes. Frank can be both: he can play his football and he can also tackle well.

My philosophy in football is that if you want to attack well then the offensive play starts from defence, and it's the same with defending: it starts from the attack. The strikers are the first line of defence, and if they are in a bad position the opposition players can come through. My ideal is to have a good footballing team all of whose players can both defend and attack, but defending is always something you can polish and improve whereas attacking football is a gift.

I know that everyone loved the flair, entertainment and excitement in our team and criticised our defence. I understand that, but it doesn't mean I have to agree with it. Because we didn't do too badly, did we? In the year and a half I was coach at Chelsea we won the FA Cup and were second in the Premiership when I left. There's always people out there ready to criticise, but they should try to appreciate the fact that I was criticising my team more than anybody else from the outside. However, sometimes I wonder whether I asked too much of my players, that we were going too quickly too soon. We needed experience but we didn't have it, and some of the players couldn't cope with the tremendous pressure that was building up – the expectancy levels were rising all the time. We would be praised if we won but criticised heavily if we lost. The players were worrying too much about making mistakes. I said to them at the start of the season, 'You are the best team in the Premiership.' But I also explained that you have to play with your head, not always your heart or your anger; you have got to be clever, and that sometimes means settling for a 1–0 win. We don't need to be searching for a 6–0 win every time we play.

A perfect example of that was our home game against Coventry. We went 1–0 down but pulled it back to 2–1 with five minutes to go. Then I saw Michael Duberry coming from the back steaming forward. What's he doing? I thought. That's just lack of experience. It is his natural enthusiasm, but there he was playing with his heart and not his head. The most important thing was to win the game, but he got carried away by thinking everyone wanted us to win in style. I would have preferred to win that game 2–1 rather than Duberry tearing away going for 3–1. Even an experienced player like Frank Leboeuf would become too enthusiastic at times. He was an exceptionally gifted player and everyone talked about him. Why? Because players in this country are labelled defenders when their only objective is to defend, but Frank could also chip the ball over a striker at forty yards' distance on to a tie – that's a Dutch expression for placing a long-range pass with such accuracy that it lands on your chest. That was more important to me. That's how I like to see attacks started, and that's the way we scored so many of our goals. But equally it is true that I wanted us to tighten up in defence and play for the result more, and that was a new phase I was devising for Chelsea. I didn't want the team to make so many mistakes, I didn't want them to be so naive. And we were working on ways to cut out our errors.

Another great player I brought to the club was Roberto Di Matteo. He scored that never-to-be-forgotten goal in the FA Cup Final. But just as important was that he was extremely consistent and outstanding throughout my time as coach at the club. Not only is he generally important to the team, he is a nice person as well. A great deal is made about certain players I've dropped, but it's easily forgotten that I also left out Roberto – only once, but nonetheless I decided to drop him. Why? I suppose he needed a rocket up his backside. And it worked – he came back with the right attitude. Again I tried to do it in a nice way by cajoling and explaining and talking to him. Then it comes down to some direct help. Roberto understood the reason for being left out and he knew I wanted to help him. When he scored at Wembley it was a great feeling for him, but it was also a great feeling for me.

A lot has been said about my goalkeepers, and I believe that signing Ed De Goey was very important, and he is a very, very good player. I had a problem in the goalkeeping position. Dmitri Kharine was a good goalkeeper but he was injured and we couldn't wait for him to recover fully. He was injured for four months and I noticed he played for the first time at Leicester when De Goey was on international duty with Holland in Florida. Frode Grodas played last season and finished with an FA Cup winners' medal, but I was very honest with him when I told him that I was not happy overall with his performance. He agreed with me. Unfortunately there is only one place in the team for a goalkeeper, and in that position you have to be 'spot on'. Yes, you can make some mistakes, but not all the time. I told him to work hard and show me in training that he could change things, but he would have to do well because I now had De Goey, Kharine and Kevin Hitchcock. I felt sorry for him but I had to tell him he was not my first choice, and eventually he went to Tottenham. I have no hard feelings about that, in fact I wish him well as I have done with all the players that have left since I've been coach. I really do hope that Frode can prove me wrong by playing well for Tottenham. It's not pleasant to have to make these sorts of decisions with players and I am not proud of it; I don't feel comfortable with it, and that's why I always hope they do well when they leave.

Naturally the player everyone wants me to talk about now is Luca Vialli. Or should I say the player manager! But now he is the coach it is a little more difficult for me, as everyone would appreciate, to discuss my relationship with him as a player. I have respect for someone like Luca Vialli, and out of respect I feel that everything I've had to say about him has already been said in any case. Of course Luca would want to show everybody that I was wrong about him. Good! That shows the character of the man. However, people can only judge those of my decisions that affected Luca in the team by results, and everyone knows the result we achieved in my first season as coach and the outstanding ones we were still achieving in my second year.

The intensity of the debate about playing Luca Vialli came from Italy. Only the Italian journalists asked at every game for which he was left out, 'Why don't you play Luca?' I understand why the Italian press had to ask questions about him all the time, but if I had left out Mark Hughes for a long period of time the English papers would have wanted to know, 'Why is an outstanding player like Mark Hughes not in the team?' I couldn't win and I would never do something just to please everybody. Whether it was perceived or not, it occurred to me that there was another issue here too: just my luck that Italy were in the same World Cup qualifying group as England. There was a sort of Cold War focused on the Bridge because Chelsea had three Italian players. It became an issue that was picked up on all the time, and it was used continually as a hook upon which to hang stories about the England–Italy World Cup games. I was stuck in the middle of it all, having played for such a long time in Italy and now pursuing a career in England. I just tried to avoid all the questions. The result was I was criticised in England for my rotation system and in Italy they said 'Ruud is rubbish' if I didn't play Luca. If I went to an Italian restaurant the question was, 'Why doesn't Vialli play?' and if I went to an ordinary restaurant in London it was 'Why isn't Dennis Wise in the team?' There was a national battle going on here. I'm Dutch, so I was neutral.

The only person that mattered in all of this was Luca Vialli, and my advice to everyone is just to look at the record books. At the point at which I left Luca was the club's top goalscorer with fifteen goals, even though I was only playing him in the games I thought would be to his advantage. Vialli was outstanding in many of the games for which I picked him. Maybe I did something right!

Now I have left Chelsea I still look for their results. My affection for the club has not dimmed, even though certain individuals have been very unfair, if not cruel, to me. Chelsea is a club still very much in my heart; I have a place in my heart for their fans and the players and that will never change. I don't want anyone at the club to worry about me. I'll get back on my feet again, I have every confidence in that.

It's a natural instinct for people to want to discuss with me Luca's team selections since I left, but I'm not thinking any more about team selection – that's not my concern. I've done all I can do for the club and I am now on the outside.

14

MY FUTURE

Ever since I left Chelsea I have been throwing all my efforts into my work on the Dutch coaching course – that's right, the one at which they said I was spending so much of my time when I was in charge at Chelsea that I was never at the training ground. What a load of nonsense that was, but now that I have little else to do it is the perfect opportunity for me to complete the course. It's like being back at school at times. I am doing all my written work, my revision and homework, and I'm thoroughly enjoying it. No one has the wisdom of football and I feel it is a valuable part of my education to learn from other coaches.

But I am back and forth all the time between Holland and England, staying at my houses in London and Amsterdam. I have a lot of interest still in England and I am quite relaxed about my future. I have got a whole lot of things to do before I settle on the next stage of my career. I still have some promotional work and photo shoots to do for my Ruud Wear collections, and I am looking forward to the World Cup Finals and my job as an ITV commentator. In the past I have enjoyed my experiences at the BBC alongside Des Lynam and Alan Hansen, Trevor Brooking and Jimmy Hill. Everybody has their own ideas, and it has been very helpful to me to hear these views. People say that Alan Hansen and I don't get along, but we have a good relationship. On screen we challenge each other's opinions, of course – that makes us interesting to watch. It makes people think about the game of football, and that is a good thing. I've always liked working with Des and I was happy for him to come over to Amsterdam to interview me the first weekend after my sacking.

I feel England will do well in France, and I have been very impressed with what has been achieved under coach Glenn Hoddle; he has developed a good team and has many innovative ideas. If I had to pick one aspect of this new England team I like the most it is the new wave of confidence that Glenn Hoddle has instilled in his players. There was an ease with which they played Italy in Rome, overcoming a World Cup qualifying tie that would in the past have caused problems. I think it was because of the new aspects Glenn Hoddle has brought to England. He has given his players a new identity, and they work very hard with each other and have a good blend. I hope he continues, but I don't know whether they are good enough actually to win the World Cup. It is unfair to put that kind of pressure on their shoulders. Of course I know so much about the England players as I have seen them nearly every week now for over two years, and I know they have a wonderful attitude to the game.

There's been a constant debate in England about the influence of foreign players – it's been a big issue ever since I arrived here. Even in Italy they are worried at the amount of foreign players in their game. The charge that is always levelled against the foreign players coming to England is that they are strangling the advancement of the young players. But I don't see that. Instead I see young players like Rio Ferdinand, Michael Owen, Robbie Fowler, Sol Campbell, Steve McManaman, David Beckham, Paul Scholes, Nicky Butt and the Neville brothers all coming through. So where is the damage being done to the young players there? I've always been convinced that youngsters can learn from top-quality foreign players and it will only serve to enhance their development. I was personally attacked for bringing so many foreign stars to Chelsea, but just look at all the young players that were in my squad as well: Jodie Morris, Nick Crittenden, Danny Granville, Mark Nichols, and even Michael Duberry.

I certainly have no regrets about my decision to come to England, despite what ultimately happened to me at Chelsea. Coming here made me a better person, enriched my experiences in life and enhanced my ideas about football. It's a vastly different game here in England and it was an adventure that I thoroughly enjoyed. The great majority of my memories are good ones.

There are exceptionally good coaches here in England – Alex Ferguson, for one. In many ways he put English football on the modern map with the style of his Manchester United team in the Champions League. Not only has he been successful but he's played in a certain way, and that is much admired throughout the rest of Europe. But it's taken him a long, long time to get it right and the club is to be applauded for having the sense to persevere with him at the beginning. When Eric Cantona left he still produced a team of flair combined with efficiency, and it has left many people asking, 'How did he do it?' It was easy: he had the experience, he knew what he was talking about, and he let his players perform without too many restrictions. He also changed his team when he had to.

Naturally I'll also be taking a keen interest in Holland's progress in the World Cup, and I think they have a very, very good team at the moment – in fact, a great team. They have every chance of being very successful. Of course the Germans will also be great competitors. Their players will be properly prepared and every aspect of their game will be spot-on. It's just incredible that all their players seem to have the right attributes: they're big, strong, athletic, can head the ball and just have the right amount of technique. It adds up to players of extraordinary talent. You've got to admire the German team spirit, they are tournament players. And I shall be looking at them very carefully.

It was a very useful exercise during Euro 96 to sit in the commentary box and watch the matches because it gave me a chance to look at players I might want to sign. I shall be doing that again during the World Cup. Just because I'm not connected with any club at the moment, don't think I won't stay up-to-date with the ins and outs of the modern game. After all, you never know what's waiting for you around the next corner.

Well, as a young boy I used to like watching *Scrooge*, so we've looked at my Christmas past, my Christmas present and my Christmas future. If I had a way of making the Christmas future better, I suppose I would like to continue to give people joy and happiness, and there are few better ways of achieving that than in sport. I hope to extend my career as long as possible.

In other ways I feel sure the extent of human knowledge will expand as it has always done, and I've a distinct feeling there will be some breakthroughs in discovering sources of energy within ourselves. Isn't it amazing that sometimes when you think of a person, at that precise moment the telephone rings and they are there? It might be telepathy or good vibes, or maybe another source of energy, who knows? I'm not a scientist, but maybe in the future there will be a way of tapping into that.

There are so many things I would like to change, perhaps too many even to discuss. Wouldn't it be nice to give people more space, make more allowances for their errors, then perhaps people would make fewer mistakes?

I used to watch *Star Trek* as a kid too, and I was always fascinated by space travel. Surely it's impossible that we are the only intellectual beings in the whole vast galaxy? Perhaps, maybe at the other end of the galaxy, if parallel worlds exist, there is some guy just like me around – perhaps he might even be an improvement, a really good player! Who knows what is out there in the universe?

Postscript
ESTELLE
AND JOELLE

Estelle has never given an interview before to any journalist. But sometimes it's difficult, if not impossible, for a man to express his innermost emotions. It's easier for a woman. Particularly for a woman close to that man. Estelle, niece of Dutch soccer legend Johan Cruyff lives with Ruud as his wife and they have a little baby girl, Joelle. As the pair sat relaxed in each other's company at their Cadogan Square apartment, just behind Peter Jones on the King's Road, they discussed their life together and their feelings after Ruud's Stamford Bridge dismissal.

Ruud: When I was sacked I turned to Estelle, as well as speaking to a lot of other people about it. I talked to Ted Troost who has helped me since I was eighteen years old. He has told me many times: 'Ruud, in this job there is a lot of stress, a lot of sharks who want things from you.' He showed

219

me how to channel my emotions professionally and he also advised me about my private life. When I was sacked I talked to him, but not in any type of consultation capacity because he knew I could handle it very well.

The most important thing in your professional life is that you must have confidence in yourself and your own ability, a belief in yourself. From my point of view I have nothing to be ashamed of after my sacking from Chelsea, and I came out of it as proudly as I went into the club. Knowing your limits and knowing your capabilities ensures that you can't be hurt that much. I was hurt for a few days, yes, but the people closest to me helped me get through it, and the person closest to me is, of course, Estelle. You are at your happiest if you are happy in your private life. And we are happy together.

Estelle: Rudi heard that he was sacked from a journalist; he then saw it on Teletext and rang me. He said: 'I believe I've been fired!' I thought it was a joke. It came as a shock because I was supposed to come back to London that Sunday, and from nowhere everything had changed.

Although it wasn't until the next day that he returned to Amsterdam, Rudi was in a trance. For about four days he was in his own world. I just couldn't believe what had happened to him because even though I don't usually get too much into football I like it when it's his club, I'm interested in his work and I was surprised that they sacked him because his team was in second place and doing very well. I might know only a little about football, but I am sure I know enough to know that doesn't make much sense. Rudi had been through it all before with other clubs but it didn't stop him being very emotional about what happened at Chelsea. He kept on saying: 'Why is it happening again?'

We organised a lot of things with my family and my friends just to get him involved so he could get it off his mind. We would go out to dinner, have a drink, go out with our friends; Rudi would go off to play golf or we'd go to parties, anything just to keep his mind occupied and stop him thinking about it.

It wasn't as if we all had time to get used to the idea. It would have been more humane to tell him and let him stay until the end of the season to get his life into order. It was just so sudden.

No, I'm not happy with what happened at Chelsea. I know a lot of people at the club and we had friends there, although maybe only a couple of friends – perhaps not as many as I thought! I would like to say who were supportive, who our true friends were at Chelsea, but now that is not easy because maybe they would be picked on at the club.

What I found very strange was that once he left, and in fact even at times when he was there, you would hear that he'd been criticised for being an arrogant person. That's not the Rudi I know. He would do more for other people than he would do for himself. That's how I can best describe him. Very caring, someone who will make more effort for other people than he would make for himself. Emotional? Yes, I would say he is, although he can't show it very much.

I didn't see him on the day he was sacked, I wasn't with him. But Rudi is not a person who cries very easily; emotional, certainly, but I don't know whether he shed any tears.

Ruud: Well, now you mention it, my friend C. J. took me to the airport after my press conference that afternoon. As I was waiting for my flight some fans came over to me. There must have been twenty of them in all but I will never forget this one guy. He had a solid silver Chelsea badge on the buttonhole of his suit. He took it off and gave it to me. He said: 'I want you to remember Chelsea for all the good times and not the bad – don't want you to ever forget Chelsea and this will remind you of the club.' My friend C. J. started crying. He said: 'I've got to leave you now, I can't stay any longer, I can't stand it anymore.' He offered me his hand but he was not looking at me, he couldn't look at me anymore, he couldn't look me in the face. The tears were rolling down his face as he walked away. That was the worst moment for me, and yes, I was very close to tears myself. I didn't feel like crying for myself, I felt sorry for my friend. I'd known C.J. ever since I was introduced to him by Andy Myers and Eddie Newton. He's a disco-bar owner who became a close friend. It's only a short journey from City airport to Amsterdam but it seemed like an eternity with my head so full of thoughts.

Estelle: He was doing so very well at Chelsea, everything was fine. There was no doubt in my mind that he wanted to stay at the club. He had decided to stay, there was no way he would have left. He stated his price for staying but there were no negotiations. He would have done the job for less – whatever had been agreed with the club he would have accepted.

Yeah, I was very happy in London and had started to settle in. Now I'm unsettled and I have to go back to Holland to be with my family and friends. Our friends and our families have helped us so much.

Ruud: There is still great disbelief. The fans are still asking questions.

Estelle: 'What is the reason?' we keep on asking ourselves. Everybody at Chelsea was so nice to your face, and while he was there everybody said to him how well he was doing. When he told me he was sacked I just thought, I'll be moving again.

We have a very strong bond. If there is something important to discuss we will talk about it and try to resolve it.

We do all kinds of things together. There are times when we are followed by photographers but it doesn't really bother me. It's really about Ruud, it's about him. And if he's happy with it so am I. Photographers spotted us some time ago going for a drink in the King's Road before we went to the cinema to watch *Men In Black*. When the film had finished I was coming down the stairs with Ruud and this girl fell to the floor in front of me. I was standing there in a state of shock as she passed out. Ruud rushed over to help and picked her up; she saw Ruud and passed out again. We carried her out of the cinema to give her some fresh air and there were photographers taking pictures, but her boyfriend wasn't very happy about it and gave one of the photographers a slap. Her boyfriend was so angry.

Ruud: Yeah, the photographers were there, but so what? I was only trying to be helpful and the girl was so grateful. Estelle called me 'Rambo Ruud'!

Estelle: I don't mind staying at home with Ruud or going out with him. We like doing things together and Ruud introduces me as his 'wife'. It's okay. Mentally, I am his wife. Marriage? Well, you never know. First we have to settle down again.

Ruud: When I first met Estelle and we first began dating, I told her all about my previous problems.

Estelle: In fact, we met a long time before that.

Ruud: You were just a little girl.

Estelle: You know he always tries to make me laugh when he keeps telling me this story that I asked him for an autograph. Did I? Well I'm not going to tell . . .

Ruud: Oh yes she did.

Estelle: When we met properly Ruud explained to me he was very suspicious about everything, especially about relation-ships. I wasn't surprised by his attitude once he told me what he had been through. Once I knew, I could cope, and our relationship began.

Ruud: Because of my two failed marriages and my children from those marriages, everything was so difficult for me.

Estelle: Yes, it amazes me even now to think about it.

Ruud: When I was telling Estelle I even thought, as I was saying it, that there must be a doubt whether she would believe any of it. But then everything I told her was verified by the people close to me, my friends and family in Italy and Holland.

Estelle: I knew women could be hard, but this was just incredible.

Ruud: I was just glad that she heard it all from other people as well.

Estelle: Parenthood? It's better than I expected. The most important thing is our personal life. If you are happy at home nothing can break you. They can sack him ten times but if he's happy at home ultimately everything will come right.

Ruud: Estelle has the body of a nineteen-year-old and the mind of a twenty-nine-year-old. It's good that I'm in such a wonderful relationship. Estelle was a great comfort to me in those early days after my dismissal at Chelsea. She was so understanding. I like being a parent. I'm very happy with my daughter. Joelle is lovely and it's great being a father again, apart from the sleepless nights. You know Joelle means 'Yes God'.

Estelle: Ruud's only joking. She sleeps right the way through. It's so easy.

Ruud: Our parents have been very supportive, Estelle's mother has been going crazy about Joelle and my mother has been very helpful and very close.

Estelle: All my friends have been very helpful as well. Life is good to us.